Grammar: Grades 1–2

Table of Contents

ISBN 978-1-60418-259-0

Ready-to-Use Ideas and Activities

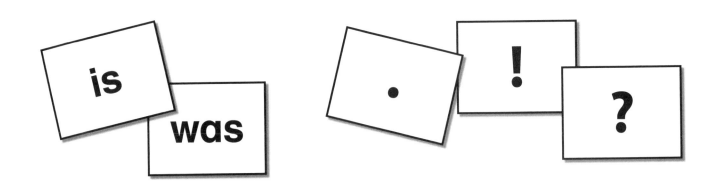

The activities in this book have been developed to help students master the basic skills necessary to succeed in grammar. These skills include learning about basic parts of speech, sentence components, and other grammar skills such as subjects and predicates. The activities have been sequenced to help ensure successful completion of the assigned tasks, thus building positive self-esteem, as well as the self-confidence students need to meet academic challenges. The activities may be used by themselves, as supplemental activities, or as enrichment material for a grammar program.

As you read through the activities listed below and go through this book, remember that all children learn at their own rate. Although repetition is important, it is critical that we keep sight of the fact that it is equally important to build children's self-esteem and self-confidence to become successful learners. If you are working with a child at home, set up a quiet, comfortable environment where you will work. Make it a special time to which you each look forward. Do only a few activities at a time and end each session on a positive note.

Flash Card Ideas

Cut apart the flash cards provided in the back of this book and use them for basic skill and enrichment activities. You can use them in the following ways or create your own way to use them.

- Write some or all of the flash card words where they can be seen and divide students into groups. As students look at the list of words, describe a word from the list. Begin with the part of speech, and then use synonyms, antonyms, spelling characteristics, a definition, how the word makes you feel, what kind of emotion it evokes, or anything else you can think of that describes the word. The team who correctly guesses the word first wins one point. After each word is guessed correctly, cross it off the list and go on to another. You can either have the group try to guess the word together or rotate guessers, giving everyone a chance. Continue playing to a certain number or until only one word remains.

Ready-to-Use Ideas and Activities

- Create a bingo sheet with five rows and five columns of blank squares. Write *FREE* in the middle square. Make enough copies to give one to each student. Write the flash card words as a list where students can see them. Have students choose 24 words from the list and write the words in the empty spaces of their bingo cards.

  When students have finished filling out their bingo cards, make the flash cards into a deck. Call out the words one at a time. If a student has the word on his card, he should mark an *X* through the word to cross it out. The student who first crosses out five words in a row—horizontally, vertically, or diagonally—wins the game when she shouts, "Bingo!"

  To extend the game, continue playing until a student crosses out all of the words on his bingo sheet.

- Give each student three or four cards. Call out a part of speech (noun, verb, adjective, etc.) and have students hold up words that belong to that category.

- Have students categorize the words into designated groups. Use the categorized groups to create sentences.

- Have students alphabetize the cards as they read the words aloud.

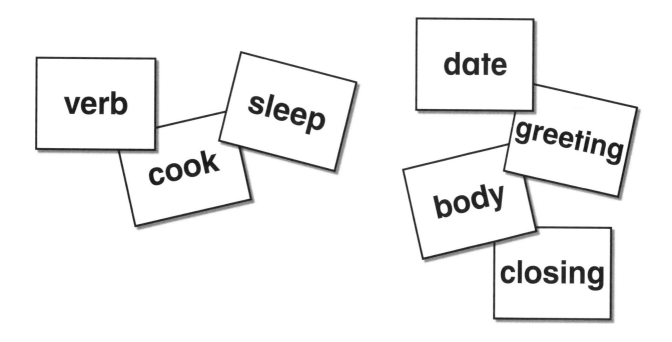

Nouns

A **noun** is a word that names a person, place, or thing.

Examples:

Person	**Place**	**Thing**
mom	park	swing
dentist	office	tooth

Write each noun in the correct column.

plate	desert	cloud
prince	store	rabbit
aunt	letter	officer
gym	city	friend

Person **Place** **Thing**

_____ _____ _____

_____ _____ _____

_____ _____ _____

_____ _____ _____

Circle the nouns in each sentence. The number tells you how many nouns there are.

1. My aunt owns a store in the country. (3)

2. The cloud is shaped like a rabbit. (2)

3. The letter is from my friend. (2)

Name _____

Nouns

A **noun** is a word that names a person, place, or thing.

Write each noun in the correct column.

glass	town	captain
kite	breeze	chief
beach	shell	kitchen
boy	dancer	station

Person   **Place**   **Thing**

_____   _____   _____

_____   _____   _____

_____   _____   _____

_____   _____   _____

Circle the nouns in each sentence. The number tells you how many nouns there are.

1. She put the glass in the kitchen. (2)

2. The kite sailed with the breeze. (2)

3. The boy found a pink and white shell at the beach. (3)

Name _____

Nouns

A **noun** is a word that names a person, place, or thing.

Write each noun in the correct column.

artist	circus	bird
forest	balloon	stepmom
paint	doctor	adult
airport	plane	library

Person	**Place**	**Thing**
_____	_____	_____
_____	_____	_____
_____	_____	_____
_____	_____	_____

Circle the nouns in each sentence. The number tells you how many nouns there are.

1. The artist likes to use blue paint. (2)

2. The plane left the airport. (2)

3. The clown at the circus gave me a balloon. (3)

Name _____

Nouns

A **noun** is a word that names a person, place, or thing.

Circle the nouns in each sentence. The number tells you how many nouns there are.

1. My grandfather drove to the store. (2)

2. The cat quickly climbed the tree. (2)

3. I have a penny in my pocket. (2)

4. The duck had a black body and a green head. (3)

5. My dad walked around the lake with our dog. (3)

6. The ground was wet from the rain. (2)

7. Please open the gate for your brother. (2)

8. My friend likes to fly a kite at the park. (3)

9. I used a paddle to row the boat. (2)

10. The fastest runner won the race. (2)

Name _____

Nouns

A **noun** is a word that names a person, place, or thing.

Circle each noun in the word box below. Some words will not be circled.

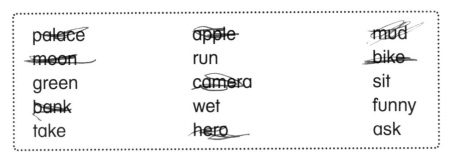

~~palace~~	~~apple~~	~~mud~~
~~moon~~	run	~~bike~~
green	~~camera~~	sit
~~bank~~	wet	funny
take	~~hero~~	ask

Write a noun in each sentence below. Use the nouns that were circled above.

1. The rain turned the dirt to __mud__ .

2. I took a picture of my family with a __camera__ .

3. The tires on the __bike__ needed air.

4. I put the money I saved in a __bank__ .

5. The __hero__ of the story was a man who helped people.

6. The king and queen live in a __palace__ .

7. I ate an __apple__ with my lunch.

8. The night sky is bright because the __moon__ is full.

Nouns

> A **noun** is a word that names a person, place, or thing.

Circle each noun in the word box below. Some words will not be circled.

baker	song	drive
barn	hold	vet
city	grow	library
skip	quiet	gift
umbrella	help	sunny

Write a noun in each sentence below. Use the nouns that were circled above.

1. The red box with a bow was a _____.

2. I used my _____ to stay dry.

3. We sang a _____ in the car.

4. The cows are in the _____.

5. We take our dog to the _____ every year.

6. I like to read at the _____.

7. The _____ sold us fresh bread.

8. I have lived in this _____ my entire life.

Proper Nouns

A **proper noun** names a specific person, place, or thing. Proper nouns begin with a capital letter.

Names given to people and pets are proper nouns.
    Example: I have a hamster named *Zeke*.

Use capital letters to write the name of each person correctly.

1. cindy lewis   _____

2. parker jones   _____

3. ms. cohen   _____

4. dan li   _____

5. mr. finley   _____

6. ellen garza   _____

Underline the proper noun in each sentence.

7. My cat Fifi likes to sleep all day.

8. Julie is my best friend.

9. I share a computer with Angelo.

10. I made a bed for my dog Spot.

Name _____

Proper Nouns

> A **proper noun** names a specific person, place, or thing. Proper nouns begin with a capital letter.
>
> Names of places are proper nouns.
>   Example: My aunt lives in *New York City.*

Use capital letters to write the name of each place correctly.

1. the corner store _____

2. miller park _____

3. jameston airport _____

4. mexico _____

5. first stop shop _____

6. los angeles, california _____

Underline the proper noun in each sentence.

7. I like to visit Jefferson Library.

8. Woodland School is where I will go next year.

9. My grandma lives in Paris, France.

10. Roberto's is my favorite place to eat.

Proper Nouns

A **proper noun** names a specific person, place, or thing. Proper nouns begin with a capital letter.

Names of specific things, such as days of the week, months, holidays, and titles, are proper nouns.

Example: *Labor Day* is always the first *Monday* in *September*.

Use capital letters to write the name of each thing correctly.

1. the animal book   _____

2. tuesday   _____

3. friday   _____

4. june   _____

5. the daily news   _____

6. canada day   _____

Underline the proper noun in each sentence.

7. My family is going to my uncle's house for Independence Day.

8. Have you read *Rhonda Goes Bananas*?

9. Tomorrow is Monday.

10. My birthday is in November.

Proper Nouns

A **proper noun** names a specific person, place, or thing. Proper nouns begin with a capital letter.

Write each noun and proper noun in the correct column.

| Thursday | April | ticket | Mexico City | Ms. Sho |
| farmer | teacher | park | Sunny Market | man |

Noun	**Proper Noun**
_____	_____
_____	_____
_____	_____
_____	_____
_____	_____

Circle the noun in each sentence. Underline the proper noun.

1. October is my favorite month.

2. The test will be on Tuesday.

3. You can hear a pin drop in Townsend Library.

4. I am reading a book called *The Whole Story.*

5. I hugged my mom on Mother's Day.

6. Beanie is a small dog.

Proper Nouns

A **proper noun** names a specific person, place, or thing. Proper nouns begin with a capital letter.

Write a proper noun to complete each sentence. Begin each proper noun with a capital letter.

People and Pets

1. My name is _____.

2. My teacher's name is _____.

3. I like spending time with my friend _____.

4. A good name for a bird is _____.

Places

5. I live in the state of _____.

6. The name of my school is _____.

7. My favorite place to eat is _____.

8. A place I would like to visit is _____.

Days, Months, Holidays, and Titles

9. My favorite day of the week is _____.

10. I like the weather in the month of _____.

11. A holiday my family takes part in is _____.

12. The next book I want to read is _____.

Name _____

Plural Nouns

> A **singular noun** names one person, place, or thing.
> Example: Lila bought one *ticket*.
>
> A **plural noun** names more than one person, place, or thing. You can make most nouns plural by adding the letter *s*.
> Example: Lila bought two *tickets*.

Write each noun in the correct column.

| peanut | toes | crickets | guitar | swing |
| band | shirts | letters | keys | pond |

Singular   **Plural**

_____   _____

_____   _____

_____   _____

_____   _____

_____   _____

Circle the correct word to finish each sentence.

1. Andrea fed each elephant one (peanut/peanuts).

2. There were three (guitar/guitars) at the store.

3. All of the (swing/swings) in the park were full.

4. Mark likes to swim in a (pond/ponds) in the summer.

Name _____

Plural Nouns

> A **plural noun** names more than one person, place, or thing.
> You can make most nouns plural by adding the letter *s*.
> Examples: cloud ⟶ clouds
> school ⟶ schools
> sister ⟶ sisters

Write each plural noun in the correct column.

birds	offices	balloons	farms
sons	dinners	kids	bakers
parks	kites	uncles	hospitals

People	**Places**	**Things**
_____	_____	_____
_____	_____	_____
_____	_____	_____
_____	_____	_____

Write the plural form of the noun at the end of each sentence.

1. The kitchen has two _____. (window)

2. Cara's party is in five _____. (day)

3. The field is full of beautiful _____. (flower)

4. Ling likes to draw _____. (shape)

Name _____

Plural Nouns

A **plural noun** names more than one person, place, or thing.
Nouns that end in *x, s, ch,* or *sh* become plural by adding *es.*
Examples: beach → beaches
ax → axes
dish → dishes
glass → glasses

Write the plural form of the noun at the end of each sentence.

1. I signed up for dance _____. (class)

2. Dad put his tools in two _____. (box)

3. Maria enjoys eating _____. (peach)

4. I gave my grandma good luck _____. (wish)

5. The spot on the shirt came out after three _____. (wash)

6. Carlos saw four _____. (fox)

7. He grew one and a half _____. (inch)

8. She bought two _____. (dress)

9. I'll give you three _____. (guess)

10. Glen helped clean the _____. (brush)

Name _____

Plural Nouns

A **plural noun** names more than one person, place, or thing.

You can make most nouns plural by adding the letter *s*.

Nouns that end in *x, s, ch,* or *sh* become plural by adding *es*.

Write each noun in the correct column.

bush	batch	pencil	bead
mix	light	toss	tiger

Add *s* to Make Plural

_____

_____

_____

_____

Add *es* to Make Plural

_____

_____

_____

_____

Circle the correct word to finish each sentence.

1. Jim cheered for two (boats/boates) in the race.

2. Lisa made a plate of (sandwichs/sandwiches) for the party.

3. I like playing (games/gamees) with friends.

4. Dad (pushs/pushes) the baby's stroller around the park.

Plural Nouns

> A **plural noun** names more than one person, place, or thing.
> You can make most nouns plural by adding the letter *s*.
> Nouns that end in *x, s, ch,* or *sh* become plural by adding *es*.

Write the plural form of each noun.

1. queen   _____

2. fork   _____

3. floss   _____

4. monkey   _____

5. branch   _____

6. ear   _____

7. speech   _____

8. fix   _____

9. ring   _____

10. nail   _____

Write the plural form of the noun in each sentence.

11. The birds in the _____ sang. (tree)

12. Frieda liked to help her uncle cook _____. (egg)

13. Peter gave two _____ about the gift. (hint)

14. Everyone sat on their _____ in the summer. (porch)

15. Many _____ have fallen from the tree. (pear)

16. I drank two _____ of water. (glass)

Plural Nouns

A **plural noun** names more than one person, place, or thing.

You can make most nouns plural by adding the letter *s*.

Nouns that end in *x, s, ch,* or *sh* become plural by adding *es*.

Solve each riddle.

1. I am made of paper, and I have two covers.

   I am a _____.

   My plural form is _____.

2. I am a round, fuzzy, and sweet fruit.

   I am a _____.

   My plural form is _____.

3. I can be made of sticks and grass, and birds live in me.

   I am a _____.

   My plural form is _____.

4. I am smooth, silver, and good for eating soup.

   I am a _____.

   My plural form is _____.

5. I am made of sand and am next to the ocean.

   I am a _____.

   My plural form is _____.

Nouns Review

Solve each riddle with a noun from the word box below.

cloud	teacher	brother
zoo	hospital	vet
library	fish	baker
school	letter	kite

People

1. I help students learn.   _____

2. I am a boy in your family.   _____

3. I make bread and sweets.   _____

4. I help animals stay well.   _____

Places

5. Students come here to learn.   _____

6. Sick people come here for special care.   _____

7. People come here to look at animals.   _____

8. There are many shelves of books here.   _____

Things

9. I look white and fluffy.   _____

10. I live in water.   _____

11. I am used to spell words.   _____

12. I fly in the sky on windy days.   _____

Nouns Review

lizard	minute	lunches	leaf
Father's Day	guards	campfire	The South Market
Monday	foxes	Ms. March	oceans

Write a singular noun from the word box to finish each sentence.

1. The game will begin in one _____.

2. I watched the _____ crawl up the tree.

3. A red _____ floated down from the tree.

4. Bob and Janell sang around the _____ for hours.

Write a plural noun from the word box to finish each sentence.

5. Seven _____ stood in front of the palace.

6. Gail has flown in an airplane over two _____.

7. James ate an apple at three _____ in a row.

8. I saw two _____ running into the forest.

Write a proper noun from the word box to finish each sentence.

9. My dad will be surprised on _____.

10. I called _____ to tell her I would be late.

11. Mom and I shop at _____ on Saturdays.

12. My favorite day is _____.

Name _____

Nouns Review

market	day	The Big Adventure	doctors
flutes	dishes	Green Park	Toto
Columbus Day	holidays	spoon	snack

Write a singular noun from the word box to finish each sentence.

1. My dad makes me a _____ after school.

2. I hold my _____ with my left hand.

3. This is the _____ I have been waiting for.

4. Grace is going to the _____ to get fruit.

Write a plural noun from the word box to finish each sentence.

5. My job is to wash the _____ after dinner.

6. There are eight _____ in the band.

7. Philip spends most _____ with his aunt and uncle.

8. Both _____ said I had the flu.

Write a proper noun from the word box to finish each sentence.

9. I am reading a book called _____.

10. Mr. Lewis likes to walk at _____.

11. Shanda named her dog _____.

12. School is out for _____.

Pronouns

A **pronoun** is a word that can take the place of a noun. *I, me, we, us, you, he, him, she, her, it, they,* and *them* are examples of pronouns.

Examples: Anna likes to run. → *She* likes to run.

Bobby enjoys soccer. → *He* enjoys soccer.

Write *he, she, it, we,* or *they* in place of the underlined words.

1. My sister and I need to water the plants.

   _____ need to water the plants.

2. The sunset was colorful.

   _____ was colorful.

3. Derek is happy because it is Monday.

   _____ is happy because it is Monday.

4. Emma and Drew watched the peacock.

   _____ watched the peacock.

5. Aunt Karen asked her friends to lunch.

   _____ asked her friends to lunch.

6. My brothers play fun games.

   _____ play fun games.

7. The red wagon has a flat tire.

   _____ has a flat tire.

8. My friends and I are in the same class.

   _____ are in the same class.

Name _____

Pronouns

A **pronoun** is a word that can take the place of a noun. *I, me, we, us, you, he, him, she, her, it, they,* and *them* are examples of pronouns.

Write *he, she, it, we,* or *they* in place of the underlined words.

1. The computer was a gift to the school.

   _____ was a gift to the school.

2. The Johnsons moved into the house next door.

   _____ moved into the house next door.

3. My dad likes to cook on the weekends.

   _____ likes to cook on the weekends.

4. Clara Barton was a nurse.

   _____ was a nurse.

5. Good friends are important.

   _____ are important.

6. Chris and I are going camping with my family.

   _____ are going camping with my family.

Write a sentence using each pronoun.

7. (I) _____

8. (You) _____

9. (We) _____

10. (They) _____

Name _____

Pronouns

A **pronoun** is a word that can take the place of a noun. *I, me, we, us, you, he, him, she, her, it, they,* and *them* are examples of pronouns.

Examples: Ann smiled at Lisa. → Ann smiled at *her*.

Celia won the race. → Celia won *it*.

Write *him, her, it, us,* or *them* in place of the underlined words.

1. Heidi wants to surprise <u>Javier</u>.

   Heidi wants to surprise _____.

2. Mom asked <u>Grandma</u> to stay at our house.

   Mom asked _____ to stay at our house.

3. The tickets are for <u>Dayton and me</u>.

   The tickets are for _____.

4. Please save seats for <u>Aisha and Lynn</u>.

   Please save seats for _____.

5. I am going to the park with <u>Uncle Jim</u>.

   I am going to the park with _____.

6. Did you hear about <u>the new bridge</u>?

   Did you hear about _____?

7. Marla needs to fix <u>her bike</u> before Friday.

   Marla needs to fix _____ before Friday.

8. Dad is spending the day with <u>my friends and me</u>.

   Dad is spending the day with _____.

Name _____

Pronouns

A **pronoun** is a word that can take the place of a noun. *I, me, we, us, you, he, him, she, her, it, they,* and *them* are examples of pronouns.

Write *him, her, it, us,* or *them* in place of the underlined words.

1. I can hear <u>your voice</u> from the back row.

   I can hear _____ from the back row.

2. What would you like <u>Anna and Bob</u> to do?

   What would you like _____ to do?

3. Marty took a picture of <u>Sarah and me</u>.

   Marty took a picture of _____.

4. Jacob handed <u>the phone</u> to me.

   Jacob handed _____ to me.

5. I made a necklace for <u>my stepmom</u>.

   I made a necklace for _____.

6. This shirt is for <u>Larry</u>.

   This shirt is for _____.

Write a sentence using each pronoun.

7. (me) _____

8. (you) _____

9. (us) _____

10. (them) _____

Name _____

Verbs

A **verb** is a word that shows action. Some verbs tell what is happening now. These verbs are called **present tense verbs**.

Examples: run   I *run* on the playground.

walk   Donna and Winston *walk* to school.

play   We *play* together.

Write the correct verb to finish each group of words.

swim	catch	win	read	eat	drive

1. _____ the food

2. _____ in the pool

3. _____ the car

4. _____ the ball

5. _____ the race

6. _____ the book

Write the correct verb to finish each sentence.

sleeps	works	rides	listens	spills	finds

7. My mom _____ to the radio in the morning.

8. Susan _____ at a store near her house.

9. Uncle Bill _____ the bus to work.

10. José _____ later on the weekends.

11. Lily _____ her juice when she is in a hurry.

12. Dad _____ pennies every place we go!

Name _____

Verbs

A **verb** is a word that shows action. Some verbs tell what is happening now. These verbs are called **present tense verbs**.

Write the correct verb to finish each group of words.

| smile | bake | plant | shop | dig | dive |

1. _____ into the pool

2. _____ a cake

3. _____ at my friend

4. _____ at the market

5. _____ a hole

6. _____ a tree

Write the correct verb to finish each sentence.

| bloom | build | march | carry | sail | sing |

7. Flowers _____ in the spring.

8. Robert and Heather _____ a boat on the lake.

9. My friends _____ in the parade each year.

10. Ants _____ food to their nest.

11. Birds _____ their nests in trees.

12. He and I _____ together in the choir.

Name _____

Verbs

A **verb** is a word that shows action. Some verbs tell what is happening now. These verbs are called **present tense verbs**.

Circle the verb in each sentence.

1. My dog Toto runs fast.

2. Erin thinks about the question.

3. He goes to class.

4. We paint pictures of flowers.

5. They climb to the top of the mountain.

6. Jim plays his guitar at lunch.

7. Henry builds snowmen during winter.

8. Hailey and I go to camp together.

9. Marie watches the parade from her window.

10. White clouds float in the blue sky.

11. The artist paints beautiful pictures.

12. He opens his eyes.

Past Tense Verbs

A **verb** is a word that can tell what is happening now or what has already happened. Verbs that tell what is happening now are **present tense verbs**. Verbs that tell what has already happened are **past tense verbs**.

Many verbs add *ed* to show the past tense.

Examples: PRESENT   walk   I *walk* to school.

PAST   walked   I *walked* to school.

Write the past tense of each verb.

1. mow   _____

2. climb   _____

3. boil   _____

4. open   _____

5. push   _____

6. fill   _____

Write the past tense of each verb to finish the story.

When I _____ Aunt Peggy last summer, we had fun. Each morning, we
        (visit)

_____ cereal and berries together for breakfast. We _____
  (mix)   (pull)

chairs onto her back porch and _____ until it was time for lunch!
                                          (talk)

At lunch, we _____ lettuce from her garden for a salad. After lunch,
                    (pick)

we _____ flowers. Then, we _____ movies at night.
     (plant)   (watch)

I _____ Aunt Peggy if I could come back this summer!
  (ask)

Name _____

Past Tense Verbs

A **verb** is a word that can tell what is happening now or what has already happened. Verbs that tell what is happening now are **present tense verbs**. Verbs that tell what has already happened are **past tense verbs**.

Many verbs add *ed* to show the past tense.

Examples: PRESENT cheer   Darrell and Hunter *cheer* at the game.

PAST   cheered   Darrell and Hunter *cheered* at the game.

Write the past tense of each verb.

1. trust _____

2. work _____

3. count _____

4. turn _____

5. lock _____

6. rest _____

Write the correct past tense verb to finish each group of words.

carried   cooked   jumped   shopped   stopped   raced

7. _____ over the puddle

8. _____ my books

9. _____ at the stop sign

10. _____ at the market

11. _____ dinner

12. _____ around the track

Past Tense Verbs

A **verb** is a word that can tell what is happening now or what has already happened. Verbs that tell what is happening now are **present tense verbs**. Verbs that tell what has already happened are **past tense verbs**.

Many verbs add *ed* to show the past tense.

Examples: PRESENT   play   Ana and Erica *play* at recess.

               PAST   played   Ana and Erica *played* at recess.

Circle the past tense verb to finish each sentence.

1. We (pick/picked) strawberries this morning.

2. I (smile/smiled) when I got my test back.

3. Mary (search/searched) for her pencil.

4. Grandma (mend/mended) the tear in my shirt.

5. We (mix/mixed) oil and vinegar to put on the salad.

Write the correct past tense verb to finish each sentence.

listened	rolled	followed	hopped	whispered

6. We _____ to the dog bark for hours.

7. Susan _____ the yarn into a ball.

8. Sam _____ like a kangaroo.

9. Melissa _____ a secret in my ear.

10. Isaac _____ the sweet smell to the bakery.

Past Tense Verbs

A **verb** is a word that can tell what is happening now or what has already happened. Verbs that tell what is happening now are **present tense verbs**. Verbs that tell what has already happened are **past tense verbs**.

Many verbs add *ed* to show the past tense.

Examples: PRESENT   wash   Andrea and Walt *wash* the car.
PAST   washed   Andrea and Walt *washed* the car.

Circle the past tense verb to finish each sentence.

1. My stepdad (stir/stirred) the soup.

2. I (watch/watched) the sun set yesterday.

3. Lynn (tie/tied) a bow on the gift.

4. My brother and I (serve/served) dinner to our mom yesterday.

5. Julie (lock/locked) the door behind her.

Write the past tense of each verb to finish the story.

Last weekend, I _____ in a soccer game. The game _____ early,
(play)   (start)

but it _____ late. Both teams _____ to win. The score
(finish)   (want)

_____ tied for almost the whole game. Our team _____ ahead and
(stay)   (push)

never _____. I think we _____ the other team! In the end, we
(rest)   (surprise)

_____ the winning goal. The crowd _____.
(kick)   (roar)

Past Tense Irregular Verbs

Some verbs use a different form of the same word to tell the past tense. These are called **irregular verbs**.

Examples: PRESENT   eat   We *eat* lunch at noon.
PAST   ate   We *ate* lunch at noon.

Draw a line to match each verb with the correct past tense form.

1. sleep   gave

2. hold   fell

3. make   left

4. win   bought

5. give   held

6. fall   made

7. buy   won

8. drink   drank

9. ride   slept

10. leave   rode

Write the past tense of each irregular verb to finish the sentence.

11. Lori _____ a card for Samantha.
(make)

12. Lindsey _____ her cat at the vet.
(hold)

13. She _____ enough bread for a week.
(buy)

14. Our team _____ the game!
(win)

Past Tense Irregular Verbs

Some verbs use a different form of the same word to tell the past tense. These are called **irregular verbs**.

Examples: PRESENT   tell   Sue and Alecia *tell* a story.

PAST   told   Sue and Alecia *told* a story.

Draw a line to match each verb with the correct past tense form.

1. fly	sang
2. swim	ran
3. sing	found
4. find	saw
5. see	caught
6. run	stood
7. catch	came
8. go	swam
9. come	went
10. stand	flew

Write the past tense of each irregular verb to finish the sentence.

11. Sylvia and I _____ the movie last night.
        (see)

12. I _____ to the gas station.
        (go)

13. You _____ just in time!
        (come)

14. John _____ his favorite song.
        (sing)

Name _____

Past Tense Irregular Verbs

Some verbs use a different form of the same word to tell the past tense. These are called **irregular verbs**.

Examples: PRESENT   sell   Pablo and Sadie *sell* cookies at the fair.

           PAST   sold   Pablo and Sadie *sold* cookies at the fair.

Write the past tense of each verb from the word box.

slid	dug	ate	fed
gave	said	told	took

1. slide   _____

2. dig   _____

3. say   _____

4. give   _____

5. take   _____

6. eat   _____

7. tell   _____

8. feed   _____

Write the past tense of each irregular verb to finish the sentence.

9. She _____ her bike to the shop.
       (take)

10. Lewis _____ lunch with Zac.
       (eat)

11. Marsha _____ her goldfish this morning.
       (feed)

12. Carla _____ a story about ice-skating.
       (tell)

Name _____

Past Tense Verbs Review

Verbs that tell what is happening now are **present tense verbs**.
Verbs that tell what has already happened are **past tense verbs**.

Write each verb in the correct column.

fall	think	ate	say
wash	tied	looked	taste
held	told	took	jump
climb	played	smile	dropped

Present   **Past**

_____   _____

_____   _____

_____   _____

_____   _____

_____   _____

_____   _____

_____   _____

_____   _____

Write the missing form of each verb.

	Present	**Past**
1.	look	_____
2.	_____	said
3.	tell	_____
4.	_____	dropped

Past Tense Verbs Review

Verbs that tell what is happening now are **present tense verbs**.
Verbs that tell what has already happened are **past tense verbs**.

Write the missing form of each verb.

	Present	Past
1.	talk	_____
2.	_____	roared
3.	_____	stopped
4.	_____	climbed
5.	follow	_____
6.	_____	ate

Write the past tense of each verb.

7. come _____

8. find _____

9. catch _____

10. plant _____

11. push _____

12. give _____

State-of-Being Verbs: *Am, Is,* and *Are*

State-of-being verbs do not show action. They tell about something that exists now or that existed in the past. *Am, is,* and *are* are examples of state-of-being verbs that tell that something exists now.

Use *am* after the word *I.*

    Example: I *am* hungry.

Use *is* to tell about one noun or pronoun.

    Examples: This *is* my shirt. Today *is* Monday.

Use *are* after the word *you* or with plural nouns and pronouns.

    Examples: You *are* a teacher. Dolphins *are* animals.

Write *am, is,* or *are* to complete each sentence.

1. My hamster _____ light brown.

2. I _____ the tallest girl on the team.

3. My lunch _____ in my backpack.

4. You _____ in line for the water fountain.

5. I _____ ready to go swimming.

6. Jonah's friends _____ laughing at a joke.

7. This candy _____ too sweet!

8. Aunt Pat _____ listening to violin music.

9. We _____ painting my room purple.

10. I _____ the president of the student council.

State-of-Being Verbs: *Am, Is,* and *Are*

State-of-being verbs do not show action. They tell about something that exists now or that existed in the past. *Am, is,* and *are* are examples of state-of-being verbs that tell that something exists now.

Write *am, is,* or *are* to complete each sentence.

1. The moon _____ bright tonight.

2. That car _____ my granddad's.

3. I _____ hungry.

4. You _____ the first person I met.

5. The trees _____ bent from the storm.

6. Seven ladybugs _____ on the window.

7. She _____ building a dollhouse.

8. Jordin _____ on time every day.

Write a sentence with the word *am*.

9. _____

Write a sentence with the word *is*.

10. _____

Write a sentence with the word *are*.

11. _____

State-of-Being Verbs: *Was* and *Were*

State-of-being verbs do not show action. They tell about something that exists now or that existed in the past. *Was* and *were* are examples of state-of-being verbs that tell that something existed in the past.

Use *was* to tell about one person, place, or thing.
    Example: I *was* hungry.

Use *were* with *you* or with more than one person, place, or thing.
    Examples: You *were* at the party. Sara and Bob *were* glad.

Write *was* or *were* to complete each sentence.

1. My window _____ open all night.

2. I _____ surprised on my birthday this year.

3. You _____ running to the library.

4. Eli _____ at the play last night.

5. Mom and Dad _____ sitting in the front row.

6. You _____ the winner!

7. They _____ able to see the ocean.

8. Jorge _____ trying to catch a fly.

9. The evening light _____ soft.

10. The clothes _____ on sale.

State-of-Being Verbs: *Was* and *Were*

> **State-of-being verbs** do not show action. They tell about something that exists now or that existed in the past. *Was* and *were* are examples of state-of-being verbs that tell that something existed in the past.

Write *was* or *were* to complete each sentence.

1. Breakfast _____ wonderful!

2. You _____ out of town.

3. Paul _____ on the bus.

4. I _____ looking the other way.

5. The movie _____ good.

6. All the monkeys _____ in one tree.

7. Ms. Mui _____ gone for a week.

8. You and I _____ on the same team.

Write a sentence with the word *was*.

9. _____

Write a sentence with the word *were*.

10. _____

Verbs: *Has* and *Have*

Some **verbs** do not show action. They tell about something that exists now or that existed in the past. *Has* and *have* are examples of verbs that tell that something exists now.

Use *has* to tell about one person, place, or thing.

    Example: She *has* blue eyes.

Use *have* with *you* and *I* and with more than one person, place, or thing.

    Examples: I *have* brown hair.

              You *have* red hair.

              Dan and Sue *have* black hair.

Write *has* or *have* to complete each sentence.

1. Sharon's apartment _____ lots of windows.

2. I _____ a dog and two cats.

3. You _____ beautiful eyes.

4. Jackie _____ many books.

5. The table _____ three legs.

6. Some houses _____ fences.

7. He _____ two sisters.

8. The cats _____ many toys.

9. Each day _____ its surprises.

10. Kelly and Mac _____ a red wagon.

Verbs: *Has* and *Have*

Some **verbs** do not show action. They tell about something that exists now or that existed in the past. *Has* and *have* are examples of verbs that tell that something exists now.

Write *has* or *have* to complete each sentence.

1. We _____ fun plans for this summer.

2. The school _____ Friday off.

3. My dad _____ three fishing poles.

4. The girl _____ a hat.

5. Lia and I _____ tomatoes on our sandwiches.

6. The doghouses _____ new roofs.

7. His sister _____ dance shoes.

8. The zoo _____ many animals.

Write a sentence with the word *has*.

9. _____

Write a sentence with the word *have*.

10. _____

Name _____

Verbs Review

> A **verb** shows an action or a state of being.

All of the words below are verbs. Circle the verbs that you have done already today. Underline the verbs that you think you will do later today.

wake	brush	eat	bake	use
laugh	hold	give	stand	jump
sit	think	talk	walk	sing
paint	climb	study	read	rest
ride	smile	skate	feed	build
play	wish	sleep	wave	swing

Write three more verbs you will do today.

_____

_____

_____

Solve each riddle with a word from the word box above.

1. I am something you do to your hair and your teeth.

    What verb am I? _____

2. I am something you can do only with your eyes closed.

    What verb am I? _____

Name _____

Adjectives

> **Adjectives** are words that describe, or tell about, nouns.
> Examples: a *good* friend   the *blue* sky
>   a *quiet* room   the *beautiful* dress

Write the best adjective to finish each group of words.

| soft | bright | loud | huge | yellow | funny |

1. the _____ clown

2. a _____ school bus

3. a _____ light

4. the _____ music

5. a _____ elephant

6. the _____ pillow

Write the best adjective to finish each sentence.

| low | warm | cute | busy | equal | tiny |

7. I put an _____ amount of soup in my bowl and yours.

8. We waited to cross the _____ street.

9. I saw a _____ bug on my desk.

10. Josie got a _____ puppy from the animal shelter.

11. It is a _____ day to wear a sweater.

12. Alice stepped over the _____ wall.

Name _____

Adjectives

Adjectives are words that describe, or tell about, nouns.
Examples: a *cute* baby   the *dry* dirt
            a *kind* boy   the *deep* hole

Write the best adjective to complete each group of words.

    famous   smooth   shiny   narrow   cool   golden

1. the _____ sun

2. a _____ rock

3. a _____ penny

4. the _____ breeze

5. a _____ path

6. a _____ person

Circle the adjective that describes the weather today.

7. Today, the weather is (warm/cool).

8. The sky is (blue/gray).

9. It is (wet/dry).

10. It is a (beautiful/cloudy) day!

Adjectives: Size and Shape

Adjectives are words that describe, or tell about, nouns.

Some adjectives describe size or shape.

Examples: SIZE   a *small* dog   a *giant* tree

SHAPE   a *square* door   a *round* window

Circle the adjectives that describe size. Underline the adjectives that describe shape.

| square | long | round | pointed | large | tall |
| giant | tiny | oval | small | wide | narrow |

Write a noun that each adjective can describe.

1. a square _____

2. a long _____

3. a round _____

4. a pointed _____

5. a large _____

6. a tall _____

7. a giant _____

8. a tiny _____

9. an oval _____

10. a small _____

11. a wide _____

12. a narrow _____

Adjectives: Color and Number

Adjectives are words that describe, or tell about, nouns.

Some adjectives describe color or number.

Examples: COLOR   a *white* fence   *blue* eyes

          NUMBER   *one* house   *many* balloons

Circle the adjectives that describe color. Underline the adjectives that describe number.

purple	green	twenty	several	some	black
gray	eleven	two	tan	fifteen	few

Write an adjective that describes color.

1. I would like a _____ shirt.

2. The room has _____ walls.

3. I am wearing _____ shoes.

4. I have _____ hair.

5. I like _____ flowers.

Write an adjective that describes number.

6. I drink about _____ glasses of water each day.

7. I sleep about _____ hours each night.

8. The room I am in has _____ windows.

9. I can think of _____ ways to say hello to someone.

10. I would like _____ apple slices after school.

Name _____

Adjectives: Senses

Adjectives are words that describe, or tell about, nouns.

Some adjectives describe how something looks, sounds, tastes, smells, or feels.

Examples: LOOKS   a *pretty* horse

SOUNDS   a *quiet* voice

TASTES   a *sweet* cookie

FEELS   a *fuzzy* rabbit

Write each adjective in the correct column.

| salty | green | rough | sweet | loud | scary |
| quiet | dark | sour | beautiful | heavy | smooth |

Looks	**Sounds**	**Tastes**	**Feels**
_____	_____	_____	_____
_____	_____	_____	_____
_____	_____	_____	_____

Write your own adjective to complete each sentence.

1. I like _____ food.

2. I like _____ music.

3. I like _____ weather.

4. I saw a _____ sunset last night.

5. I heard a _____ whistle.

6. I felt a _____ tap on my shoulder.

Adjectives After State-of-Being Verbs

Adjectives are words that describe, or tell about, nouns.

Sometimes, adjectives come after the state-of-being verbs *am, is, are, was,* and *were.*

    Examples: I am *tired.*   The house is *red.*   People are *funny.*

                 Paul was *early.*   You were *glad.*

Write the best adjective to complete each sentence.

fun	noisy	nice	cool	warm

1. Camping is _____.

2. The sunshine feels _____.

3. The river is _____.

4. The tree frogs are _____.

5. The people we meet are _____.

Write your own adjective to finish each sentence.

6. Spring was _____ this year.

7. Winter usually is _____.

8. The last few summers were _____.

9. Leaves are _____ in autumn.

10. Each season is _____.

Adjectives After State-of-Being Verbs

> **Adjectives** are words that describe, or tell about, nouns.
>
> Sometimes, adjectives come after the state-of-being verbs *am, is, are, was,* and *were.*

Write the best adjective to complete each sentence.

hungry	happy	helpful	long	full

1. He was _____ to go to school.

2. I was _____ for lunch.

3. The people at the bank were _____.

4. The line for movie tickets was _____.

5. The glass was _____.

Write your own adjective to complete each sentence.

6. Butterflies are _____.

7. A grasshopper is _____.

8. Flies are _____.

9. A ladybug is _____.

10. Ants are _____.

Adjectives Review

Adjectives are words that describe, or tell about, nouns.

Circle the adjective in each group of words. Underline the noun that it describes.

1. a colorful sunset

2. a sour grapefruit

3. the fast bike

4. the brown dog

5. a fluffy pillow

6. twelve kangaroos

7. my little toe

8. the green grasshopper

9. a round orange

10. my new shoes

11. a good book

12. the bright moon

13. the big game

14. your funny jokes

15. a narrow road

16. a happy puppy

17. the young cat

18. the happy news

Name _____

Adjectives Review

Circle the adjective that describes each underlined noun.

1. I helped plant a beautiful <u>garden</u> at my school.

2. The <u>dirt</u> was rocky, so we added soil.

3. We planted tomato plants in five <u>rows</u>.

4. We will pick them when <u>they</u> are ripe.

5. Then, we will make a tasty <u>sauce</u> for spaghetti.

Circle two adjectives that describe each underlined noun.

6. I have a blue and green <u>coat</u>.

7. <u>It</u> is big and warm.

8. My mom made the coat from old, colorful <u>sweaters</u>.

9. It is my special winter <u>coat</u>.

10. I wear it every cold <u>day</u>.

Circle all of the adjectives in each sentence. The number tells you how many there are.

11. I am helping my dad build a new doghouse for Bingo. (1)

12. He asked me to bring him four long nails and one hammer. (3)

13. He asked me to draw a round shape for the door and two squares for windows. (2)

14. We worked all day on a sunny Saturday and finished. (1)

15. Bingo is happy, and my dad and I are tired! (2)

Name _____

Adjectives That Compare

> You can compare two nouns by adding *er* to many adjectives. You can compare more than two nouns by adding *est* to many adjectives.
>
> Examples: Lucy is *taller* than Lara.
>
> Nina is the *tallest* girl in the class.

Write *er* at the end of each adjective to compare the two things in each sentence.

1. Tom's kitten is _____ than Steve's kitten.
   (old)

2. February is usually _____ than March.
   (cold)

3. My pillow is _____ than my sister's pillow.
   (soft)

4. Cloudy nights are _____ than clear nights.
   (dark)

5. Mindy's dinner is _____ than Lupe's dinner.
   (warm)

Write *est* at the end of each adjective to compare the things in each sentence.

6. Rhode Island is the _____ state in the United States.
   (small)

7. The red car is the _____ on the track.
   (fast)

8. This is the _____ weather that we have had this month.
   (cool)

9. That apple is the _____ in the tree.
   (high)

10. Your smile is the _____ one I have seen!
    (bright)

Name _____

Adjectives That Compare

You can compare two nouns by adding *er* to many adjectives. You can compare more than two nouns by adding *est* to many adjectives.

Examples: Autumn is *colder* than summer.

Winter is the *coldest* time of year.

Write the missing form of each word.

	Compares Two Things	**Compares More Than Two Things**
1.	longer	_____
2.	_____	tallest
3.	warmer	_____
4.	_____	shortest
5.	_____	fastest
6.	_____	highest
7.	sharper	_____
8.	cooler	_____
9.	_____	oldest
10.	younger	_____

Write a sentence comparing two things.

11. _____

Write a sentence comparing more than two things.

12. _____

Articles

A, an, and the are a special kind of adjective called **articles**. They help nouns.

A is used before a noun that begins with a consonant.
   Example: a beetle

An is used before a noun that begins with a vowel.
   Example: an ant

The is used before a noun that names a particular person, place, or thing.
   Example: the bear

Write a or an for each noun.

1. _____ forest

2. _____ plant

3. _____ umbrella

4. _____ elevator

5. _____ arrow

6. _____ gallon

7. _____ triangle

8. _____ oar

9. _____ idea

10. _____ newspaper

Write a, an, or the to finish each sentence.

11. Miriam and Todd walked to _____ pond.

12. They saw _____ lizard running up a tree.

13. They saw a fish swimming in _____ water.

14. Todd got hungry and took _____ apple out of his bag.

15. Miriam ate _____ banana.

Articles

A, an, and *the* are a special kind of adjective called **articles**. They help nouns.

A is used before a noun that begins with a consonant.
    Example: *a* chair

An is used before a noun that begins with a vowel.
    Example: *an* egg

The is used before a noun that names a particular person, place, or thing.
    Example: *the* woman

Write *a* or *an* for each noun.

1. _____ zipper

2. _____ owl

3. _____ itch

4. _____ dish

5. _____ brother

6. _____ clown

7. _____ airplane

8. _____ oven

9. _____ sale

10. _____ actor

Write a sentence with *a*.

11. _____

Write a sentence with *an*.

12. _____

Write a sentence with *the*.

13. _____

Parts of Speech Review

Write a word that fits each description.

1. verb (past tense)

_____

2. proper noun (title of a book)

_____

3. adjective (sense)

_____

4. proper noun (name of a person)

_____

5. noun (place)

_____

6. verb (now)

_____

7. noun (thing, plural)

_____

8. adjective (number more than one)

_____

9. adjective (color)

_____

10. noun (person)

_____

11. adjective (after state-of-being verb)

_____

**Write the words from the numbers above to complete the story below.
Read your story to a friend.**

A Kind Gorilla

I just (1)_____ a book called (2)_____. It was about a

(3)_____ gorilla named (4)_____. In the story, the gorilla

lives in a (5)_____. The gorilla (6)_____ all day and eats

(7)_____ off the trees. One day, the gorilla finds (8)_____

(9)_____ kittens that are lost. The gorilla helps the kittens find their

(10)_____. In the end, everyone is (11)_____.

Name _____

Parts of Speech Review

For each sentence, write *N* if the underlined word is a noun, *V* if it is a verb, *A* if it is an adjective, or *P* if it is a pronoun.

_____ 1. Mary had a <u>little</u> lamb.

_____ 2. The cow <u>jumped</u> over the moon.

_____ 3. He lives on <u>Drury Lane</u>.

_____ 4. Jack and Jill <u>went</u> up the hill.

_____ 5. The less <u>he</u> spoke, the more he heard.

_____ 6. An apple a day keeps the <u>doctor</u> away.

_____ 7. The ants go marching <u>one</u> by one.

_____ 8. How does your <u>garden</u> grow?

Circle the adjective that describes the underlined noun.

9. We sing a quiet <u>song</u> before bed.

10. My stepmom wishes me sweet <u>dreams</u>.

11. Sometimes, Dad tells short <u>stories</u>.

12. I get into my warm <u>bed</u> and go to sleep.

Write the sentence in number 9 in the past tense.

13. _____

Write the sentence in number 10 in the past tense.

14. _____

Write the sentence in number 11 with a pronoun.

15. _____

Name _____

Sentences

A **sentence** is a group of words that tells a complete idea.
    Example: Sentence   We traveled around the United States.
           Not a sentence   Around the United States.

Write _S_ if the words below make a sentence. Write _NS_ if they do not make a sentence.

_____ 1. We went to Texas.

_____ 2. Saw the Alamo in San Antonio.

_____ 3. Colorado is a beautiful state.

_____ 4. Tall mountains and cool air.

_____ 5. I would like to live there.

_____ 6. We also saw California.

_____ 7. The beautiful ocean.

Write words of your own to complete each sentence.

8. This summer, _____

_____.

9. Our dog Bingo _____

_____.

10. One day, _____

_____.

Sentences

A **sentence** is a group of words that tells a complete idea.
Example: Sentence   Our tennis team won the match.
          Not a sentence   Our tennis team.

Draw a line to match the beginning of each sentence on the left with the correct end of each sentence on the right.

1. Basketball   make a basket.

2. Two teams   the most points wins.

3. Each team   is fun.

4. You try to   play each other.

5. The team with   has five players.

Write words of your own to complete each sentence.

6. The sport _____

_____.

7. My team _____

_____.

8. During one game, _____

_____.

9. After the game, _____

_____.

Word Order

> Changing the order of words in a sentence can change the meaning of the sentence.
>
>   Example: Sue is shorter than Carmen.
>   Carmen is shorter than Sue.
>
> These sentences have the same words, but they mean different things.

Draw a picture of each sentence.

1. A circle is on top of a square.

   A square is on top of a circle.

2. A star is to the left of the moon.

   The moon is to the left of a star.

3. Kayla is taller than Jake.

   Jake is taller than Kayla.

Word Order

Changing the order of words in a sentence can change the meaning of the sentence.

Example: The chair is on the floor.
           The floor is on the chair.

These sentences have the same words, but they mean different things. If the words are not in the correct order, sometimes the sentence does not make sense.

Circle the sentence in each pair that makes sense.

1. The straw is in the glass.   The glass is in the straw.

2. Please put the deck on the plant.   Please put the plant on the deck.

3. Angelo came to my house.   My house came to Angelo.

4. I went to the party early.   I went to party the early.

5. The desk is on the lamp.   The lamp is on the desk.

6. Please phone the answer.   Please answer the phone.

7. A bird sang a song.   A song sang a bird.

8. The stairs go to the classrooms.   The classrooms go to the stairs.

9. I am going to dog the walk.   I am going to walk the dog.

10. Lawn is good for the rain.   Rain is good for the lawn.

Name _____

Declarative Sentences

A **declarative sentence** makes a statement. Declarative sentences begin with a capital letter and end with a period (.).

Examples: Statements   I bought bread at the bakery.
                                    I carried the bread in a basket.

              Not Statements   Did you get the bread at the bakery?
                                    How will you carry it home?

Write S for each sentence that makes a statement. Write NS for each sentence that does not make a statement.

_____ 1. The baker is Ms. Smith.

_____ 2. She bakes bread and cookies.

_____ 3. Does anyone help her?

_____ 4. A boy named Sam helps her.

_____ 5. Is the bread baked every day?

_____ 6. How much does it cost?

_____ 7. She makes some bread with cinnamon.

_____ 8. The bread smells good.

Write each declarative sentence with a capital letter and a period.

9. the ocean is deep _____

10. some parts are a mystery _____

11. some mammals live in the ocean _____

_____

12. a lot is unknown _____

Name _____

Declarative Sentences

A **declarative sentence** makes a statement. Declarative sentences begin with a capital letter and end with a period (.).

Examples: Statements   I like to run and play.

Amad plays baseball with me.

Not Statements   Do you like to run?

Who plays with you?

Write S for each sentence that makes a statement. Write NS for each sentence that does not make a statement.

_____ 1. Exercise is good for your heart.

_____ 2. Do you exercise?

_____ 3. You could swim.

_____ 4. Some people like to run.

_____ 5. Have you tried karate?

_____ 6. What do you like to do?

_____ 7. You can exercise before school.

_____ 8. Exercise is fun.

Write each declarative sentence with a capital letter and a period.

9. i like running in autumn _____

10. the leaves are colorful _____

11. the air is cool _____

12. i stretch before and after I run _____

_____

Declarative Sentences

A **declarative sentence** makes a statement. Declarative sentences begin with a capital letter and end with a period (.).

Examples: Statements   Mario likes to ride in airplanes.
Tim likes to ride in the car.

Not Statements   What do you like to ride in?
Where do you like to go?

Write _S_ for each sentence that makes a statement. Write _NS_ for each sentence that does not make a statement.

_____ 1. Earth has seven big areas of land.

_____ 2. The largest continent is called Asia.

_____ 3. Which is the smallest?

_____ 4. One continent is too cold for people to live.

_____ 5. How cold is it?

_____ 6. Many people live in Asia.

_____ 7. Where do you live?

_____ 8. The United States is part of North America.

Write each declarative sentence with a capital letter and a period.

9. i enjoy going to new places _____

10. i always bring my camera _____

Write your own statement with a capital letter and a period.

11. _____

_____

Interrogative Sentences

An **interrogative sentence** asks a question. An interrogative sentence begins with a capital letter and ends with a question mark (?).

Examples: What did you have for lunch?

Did you have a sandwich?

Write *Q* for each sentence that asks a question. Write *NQ* for each sentence that does not ask a question.

_____ 1. What time do you eat lunch?

_____ 2. Jerry ate a pickle.

_____ 3. Who ate an orange?

_____ 4. Lunch is my favorite meal.

_____ 5. Where is the lunchroom?

_____ 6. Do you smell the pie?

_____ 7. What kind of vegetable is this?

_____ 8. Please set the table.

Write each interrogative sentence with a capital letter and a question mark.

9. do we eat lunch at noon

_____

10. should i bring my lunch

_____

11. can Jephta buy her lunch

_____

12. will we sit at the same table

_____

Interrogative Sentences

An **interrogative sentence** asks a question. An interrogative sentence begins with a capital letter and ends with a question mark (?).

     Examples: Who is playing the piano?

                 Is Tim singing?

Write *Q* for each sentence that asks a question. Write *NQ* for each sentence that does not ask a question.

_____ 1. Are you in the band?

_____ 2. Collin plays the flute.

_____ 3. Who plays the drums?

_____ 4. Have you heard of Buddy Holly?

_____ 5. Do you like music?

_____ 6. A piano has 88 keys.

_____ 7. Does a violin have four strings?

_____ 8. Lisa plays electric guitar.

Write each interrogative sentence with a capital letter and a question mark.

9. what kind of music do you like

_____

10. do you sing

_____

11. can you make music with a spoon

_____

12. is Katie in a band

_____

Interrogative Sentences

An **interrogative sentence** asks a question. An interrogative sentence begins with a capital letter and ends with a question mark (?).

      Examples: Which color do you like best?

                  Who is painting?

Write *Q* for each sentence that asks a question. Write *NQ* for each sentence that does not ask a question.

_____ 1. Do you like to draw?

_____ 2. What do you draw?

_____ 3. I like to use a pencil.

_____ 4. Do you have colored pencils?

_____ 5. Will you show me how to draw?

_____ 6. I want to draw a horse.

_____ 7. Is drawing easy for you?

_____ 8. Which pencil is yours?

Write each interrogative sentence with a capital letter and a question mark.

9. does John like to paint

_____

10. which color is his favorite

_____

Write your own interrogative sentence with a capital letter and a question mark.

11. _____

_____

Exclamatory Sentences

An **exclamatory sentence** shows strong feeling. It starts with a capital letter and ends with an exclamation mark (!). Some exclamatory sentences are only one or two words long.

Examples: Wow!

What a great movie!

Write *E* for each sentence that shows strong feeling. Write *NE* for each sentence that does not show strong feeling.

_____ 1. You are doing a great job!

_____ 2. That is a nice shirt.

_____ 3. There is a mouse!

_____ 4. Is the wind blowing?

_____ 5. Boo!

Write each exclamatory sentence with a capital letter and an exclamation mark.

6. ouch

_____

7. what an amazing sunset

_____

8. this is the best soup ever

_____

Exclamatory Sentences

> An **exclamatory sentence** shows strong feeling. It starts with a capital letter and ends with an exclamation mark (!). Some exclamatory sentences are only one or two words long.
>
> Examples: Hooray!
>
> You did a great job!

Write *E* for each sentence that shows strong feeling. Write *NE* for each sentence that does not show strong feeling.

_____ 1. What did they say?

_____ 2. It is a boy!

_____ 3. Thank you for the card.

_____ 4. I am so happy for you!

_____ 5. That is wonderful news!

Write each exclamatory sentence with a capital letter and an exclamation mark.

6. watch out

_____

7. i had a great day

_____

Write your own exclamatory sentence with a capital letter and an exclamation mark.

8. _____

_____

Name _____

Imperative Sentences

An **imperative sentence** gives a command. An imperative sentence can end in an exclamation mark (!) or a period (.).
Examples: Clean your room!
Be good.

Write *I* for each sentence that gives a command. Write *NI* for each sentence that does not give a command.

_____ 1. It is time to wake up.

_____ 2. Put on your clothes.

_____ 3. Breakfast is ready.

_____ 4. Can you be ready in five minutes?

_____ 5. Remember your homework!

_____ 6. The bus leaves soon.

_____ 7. Have a good day!

_____ 8. When will you be home?

Draw a line to match the words on the left with the words on the right to make imperative sentences.

9. Remember   a good job!

10. Be   your umbrella.

11. Find   nice!

12. Do   your seat, please.

Imperative Sentences

An **imperative sentence** gives a command. An imperative sentence can end in an exclamation mark (!) or a period (.).

Examples: Pick up your toys.

Look out!

Write *I* for each sentence that gives a command. Write *NI* for each sentence that does not give a command.

_____ 1. Show your mom your painting.

_____ 2. She will love it!

_____ 3. Tell her how you made it.

_____ 4. Has your dad seen it?

_____ 5. Make him a painting.

_____ 6. You could make a card.

_____ 7. Cards are great gifts.

_____ 8. Get started!

Draw a line to match the words on the left with the words on the right to make imperative sentences.

9. Start   out the trash.

10. Take   your best.

11. Do   moving!

12. Sit,   Bingo!

Sentences Review

Write *D* if the sentence is declarative, *IN* if it is interrogative, *E* if it is exclamatory, or *IM* if it is imperative.

_____ 1. Do you have any pets?

_____ 2. I have a cat.

_____ 3. Where does your cat like to sleep?

_____ 4. She likes to sleep on my feet!

_____ 5. That is funny!

_____ 6. Sometimes, she plays with my toes.

_____ 7. She is playful.

_____ 8. Ouch!

_____ 9. Please settle down, Kitty!

_____ 10. I feed my cat every morning.

_____ 11. Does she drink milk?

_____ 12. No, she does not drink milk.

Write one declarative sentence, one interrogative sentence, one exclamatory sentence, and one imperative sentence.

13. Sometimes, _____

14. Have you _____

15. Wow, _____

16. Remember _____

Subjects

> The **subject** of a sentence tells who or what the sentence is about.
> Examples: *Spring* is a pretty time of year.
> *Some leaves* turn red in autumn.

Circle the subject of each sentence.

1. Flowers bloom in the spring.

2. The rain helps things grow.

3. Baby animals are born.

4. Summer is the warmest season.

5. People like to play in the sun.

6. A cool breeze blows in autumn.

7. Red and gold leaves fall from the trees.

8. Winter is cold.

9. People and animals stay at home in the winter.

Write a subject to complete each sentence.

> Jackets and hats   Autumn   I

10. _____ is my favorite season.

11. _____ like cool weather.

12. _____ are fun to wear.

Subjects

The **subject** of a sentence tells who or what the sentence is about.
Examples: *Birds* are flying in the sky.
The cat is sleeping.

Circle the subject of each sentence.

1. Katie saw a book on a chair.

2. She took the book to her teacher.

3. Her teacher asked the class about the book.

4. Nobody was missing the book.

5. Rick and Tina walked with Katie to the office.

6. The lost-and-found box was in the office.

7. They gave the book to an office helper.

8. The office helper was happy.

9. The book was his!

Write a subject to complete each sentence.

Mr. Thomas   Mystery stories   He

10. _____ is the office helper.

11. _____ likes to read at lunch.

12. _____ are his favorite books.

Subjects

The **subject** of a sentence tells who or what the sentence is about.
Examples: *Bo and Mary* walked to the park.
A dog ran by them.

Draw a picture of the subject of each sentence.

1. The telephone rang twice before Ann answered.

2. The sun is bigger than the moon.

3. Rita and Javier are in the band at Jefferson School.

4. Bananas taste better than apples.

5. Five pennies equal a nickel.

Subjects Review

> The **subject** of a sentence tells who or what the sentence is about.
> Examples: *Mom* is painting a picture.
> *Dad* is cooking dinner.

Circle the subject of each sentence.

1. I helped Grandma make vegetable soup.

2. We washed all the vegetables.

3. The pot was on the stove.

4. The carrots were put in the pot first.

5. We put salt in last.

6. My bowl was empty fast!

Write a subject from the box to complete each sentence.

> Grandma   Her soups   We

7. _____ is a super cook.

8. _____ make good meals together.

9. _____ taste wonderful.

Draw a picture of the subject of the sentence.

10. Hot soup is good in the winter.

Predicates

The **predicate** of a sentence tells something about the subject.
Examples: Yellow *is Jonah's favorite color.*
His room *is yellow.*

Underline the predicate of each sentence.

1. A kangaroo has a pouch.

2. Peacocks have colorful feathers.

3. A parrot can talk.

4. A crow is black.

5. A robin is red.

6. Ladybugs are small.

7. Penguins like snow and ice.

8. Monkeys hang from trees.

9. Dolphins live in the ocean.

Write a predicate from the box to complete each sentence.

have long tails   are fish   hop

10. Sharks _____.

11. Frogs _____.

12. Horses _____.

Name _____

Predicates

The **predicate** of a sentence tells something about the subject.
Examples: The ball *is black and white.*
Players *kick the ball to score.*

Underline the predicate of each sentence.

1. Brad plays soccer.

2. He is on a team with his friends.

3. His team wins a lot of games.

4. Sometimes, they lose games.

5. They played a big game on Saturday.

6. Brad wanted to win.

7. The other team was good.

8. Both teams played hard.

9. The teams tied!

Write a predicate from the box to complete each sentence.

are on her team   play on Thursday   plays basketball

10. Sarah _____.

11. Her friends _____.

12. Next week, they _____.

Predicates

The **predicate** of a sentence tells something about the subject.
Examples: Blue *is my favorite color.*
The picture *is on the wall.*

Underline the predicate of each sentence.

1. Nicole wants to paint her room.

2. She likes the color green.

3. Dad told Nicole she could paint her room.

4. He said that he would help.

5. They bought green paint.

6. Nicole and Dad went home.

7. They had brushes.

8. Nicole's room was green soon.

9. It was beautiful!

Write a predicate from the box to complete each sentence.

| likes the color orange | is a nice color too | is painted blue |

10. Brett _____.

11. His room _____.

12. Blue _____.

Predicates Review

Underline the predicate of each sentence. Write it on the line.

1. My family went on a trip.

   _____

2. We packed the car.

   _____

3. My mom and dad drove.

   _____

4. My brother and I sang songs in the backseat.

   _____

5. We all had fun.

   _____

Write your own predicate to finish each sentence.

6. The huge elephant _____.

7. A rose _____.

8. My shoes _____.

9. Butterflies _____.

10. In the summer, I _____.

Capitalization

> The first word in a sentence begins with a **capital letter**.
>   Examples: The cat is orange and white.
>   An apple is round.
>
> A person's title and his or her first and last name should begin with a **capital letter**.
>   Examples: Chris Parker
>   Ms. Lewis

Circle each letter that needs to be capitalized.

1. My friends jane smith and jody horton are in my class.

2. our teacher is mr. cole.

3. Today, I went to see dr. collier.

4. this jacket belongs to mary jo gosdin.

5. has anyone seen jack, jr., today?

6. My mom called aunt susan yesterday.

Answer each question with a person's name.

7. Who is your teacher? _____

8. Who is one of your friends? _____

9. Who is your neighbor? _____

10. Who do you know owns a dog? _____

Name _____

Capitalization

Days, months, and names of cities, states, and provinces should begin with a **capital letter**.

Examples: Friday, October 12

Portland, Oregon

Circle each letter that needs to be capitalized.

1. School starts on september 2 this year.

2. My favorite day is tuesday.

3. We visited austin, texas, in may.

4. Brian lives in new york city, new york.

5. On wednesday, december 9, we will see a play.

6. Next monday is my birthday.

Answer each question with a day, month, or name of a city or state.

7. When is your birthday?_____

8. What town or city do you live in? _____

9. What is today? _____

10. Where would you like to visit? _____

Capitalization

> The first word and all important words in book and movie titles should begin with a **capital letter**.
>
> Examples: *The Magic School Bus*
> *Dictionary of Animals*

Circle each letter that needs to be capitalized.

1. the little red engine

2. lily goes to rome

3. playing the guitar

4. guide to dinosaurs

5. learn to make a kite

6. bingo chases sticks

Answer each question with a book or movie title.

7. What is your favorite book? _____

8. What is your favorite movie? _____

9. What book are you reading now? _____

10. What was the last movie you saw? _____

Capitalization Review

Circle each letter that needs to be capitalized.

1. Our school has friday off.

2. i am reading a book called <u>saving the ocean</u>.

3. I would like to visit boulder, colorado.

4. will mr. nelson be there?

5. the talent show is on july 22.

6. I am glad that jason floyd and ashley harris will be there.

7. This letter will go to spring, arizona.

8. my sister's birthday is january 23.

Answer each question.

9. What country do you live in? _____

10. Who is sitting next to you? _____

11. When is your teacher's birthday? _____

12. What is a book about an animal? _____

Name _____

Ending Punctuation

Every sentence ends with a **punctuation mark**.

A declarative sentence ends with a **period**.
   Example: My name is Sherry.

An interrogative sentence ends with a **question mark**.
   Example: What is your name?

An exclamatory sentence ends with an **exclamation mark**.
   Example: Here I am!

An imperative sentence ends with either a period or an exclamation mark.
   Examples: Please close the window.
                      Wow!

Write the correct ending punctuation mark for each sentence.

1. The sky is getting dark___

2. Can I watch your game___

3. I cannot believe it___

4. You found me___

5. Will you be at the party___

6. Tina is taking a dance class___

7. Laura is my older sister___

8. The clock has stopped___

9. What do you want for dinner___

10. Not again___

11. This is easy___

12. The lettuce is fresh___

13. Do you want to play a game___

14. What a beautiful song___

Ending Punctuation

A declarative sentence ends with a **period**.

An interrogative sentence ends with a **question mark**.

An exclamatory sentence ends with an **exclamation mark**.

An imperative sentence ends with either a **period** or an **exclamation mark**.

Write the correct ending punctuation mark for each sentence.

1. What size shoe do you wear___

2. The kitchen is painted yellow___

3. When will you be home___

4. I cannot carry this box much longer___

5. Do you have a pencil___

6. The parrot repeated what Lucy said___

7. We need an umbrella right now___

8. Ida likes to sleep with the fan on___

9. Did you find this shell at the beach___

10. What fun___

11. What did you think of the movie___

12. I would like some water___

13. Artie went for a walk___

14. I counted over 100 bees___

Contractions

A **contraction** is made when two words are put together. Letters are taken out and an apostrophe is put in their place.

Examples: does + not = *doesn't*

would + not = *wouldn't*

Some contractions do not follow this rule.

Example: will + not = *won't*

Match each word with its contraction.

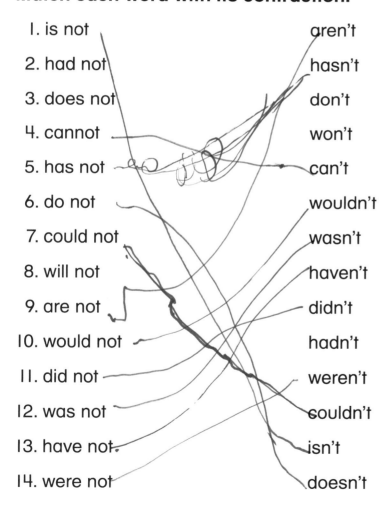

1. is not	aren't
2. had not	hasn't
3. does not	don't
4. cannot	won't
5. has not	can't
6. do not	wouldn't
7. could not	wasn't
8. will not	haven't
9. are not	didn't
10. would not	hadn't
11. did not	weren't
12. was not	couldn't
13. have not	isn't
14. were not	doesn't

Contractions

A **contraction** is made when two words are put together. Letters are taken out and an apostrophe is put in their place.

Some contractions are made with a pronoun + a verb.

Examples: she + will = *she'll*   I + am = *I'm*

he + is = *he's*   we + are = *we're*

Match each word with its contraction.

1. they are   she'll

2. you are   they're

3. she is   we're

4. it is   he's

5. I am   he'll

6. they will   she's

7. he is   they'll

8. she will   you're

9. we are   it's

10. he will   I'm

Write the contraction for each group of words.

11. you are = _____

12. he will = _____

13. I am = _____

14. it is = _____

Contractions

A **contraction** is made when two words are put together.
Letters are taken out and an apostrophe is put in their place.

Write the contraction for each word or group of words.

1. cannot = _____

2. they are = _____

3. do not = _____

4. will not = _____

5. she is = _____

Write a contraction to finish each sentence.

6. She _____ know what time it was.
   (did not)

7. Tom _____ go to the game.
   (cannot)

8. I think _____ going to need a coat today.
   (I am)

9. You _____ believe it!
   (will not)

10. It sounds like _____ not feeling well.
    (you are)

11. Please _____ slip on the ice!
    (do not)

12. Vonda says _____ time to go home.
    (it is)

Contractions

> A **contraction** is made when two words are put together. Letters are taken out and an apostrophe is put in their place.

Write the contraction for each group of words.

1. is not = _____

2. does not = _____

3. would not = _____

4. he is = _____

5. she will = _____

Write a contraction to complete each sentence.

6. We _____ seen the movie.
          (have not)

7. Ryan _____ able to visit Aunt Anne.
          (was not)

8. He said _____ be there at 2:00 p.m.
          (he will)

Write your own sentence with the contraction for each word or group of words.

9. cannot: _____

_____

10. will not: _____

_____

Possessives

A **possessive** word tells who or what owns something. To make a word possessive, you add an apostrophe and the letter *s*.

Examples: The book's cover is pink. → the cover belongs to the book

Mary's shoe has a bow. → the shoe belongs to Mary

Write the possessive form of each word.

1. Mark _____

2. uncle _____

3. grandmother _____

4. city _____

5. boat _____

6. Kate _____

7. child _____

8. flower _____

Write the possessive form of the word to complete each sentence.

9. The _____ flame was orange.
(candle)

10. I read _____ story.
(Andy)

11. The _____ peel was tough.
(fruit)

12. Sasha likes the _____ laugh.
(character)

Possessives

> A **possessive** word tells who or what owns something. To make a word possessive, you add an apostrophe and the letter *s*.

Use a possessive to say the same thing as each group of words. The first one has been done for you.

1. the bag of Nora ___**Nora's bag**_____

2. the color of the hat _____

3. the leg of the chair _____

4. the feathers of the chicken _____

5. the lunch of Harry _____

6. the edge of the road _____

7. the corner of the table _____

8. the luck of the beginner _____

9. the taste of the blueberry _____

10. the wheel of the bicycle _____

11. the aquarium of the fish _____

12. the class of the teacher _____

13. the refrigerator of Ali _____

14. the bark of the dog _____

15. the toothpaste of Ned _____

Possessives

A **possessive** word tells who or what owns something. To make a word possessive, you add an apostrophe and the letter *s*.

Use a possessive to say the same thing as each group of words. The first one has been done for you.

1. the shape of the cloud **the cloud's shape** _____

2. the ring of the telephone _____

3. the talent of the actor _____

4. the eyes of the toad _____

5. the sound of the bell _____

6. the floor of the ocean _____

Write the possessive form of the word to complete each sentence.

7. Please read _____ letter.
        (Thea)

8. That is the _____ paint.
        (artist)

9. The _____ fur was brown.
        (bear)

10. The _____ ink was blue.
        (pen)

Write a sentence with each possessive word.

11. Todd's: _____

12. mouse's: _____

Proofreading

Reading your sentences to check for mistakes is called **proofreading**. Check for mistakes in spelling, capital letters, and punctuation marks.

Example: Before proofreading   Vanessa and bill are swingin (3 mistakes)

Corrected   Vanessa and Bill are swinging.

Each sentence has an incorrect or missing capital letter. Draw a circle around the letter that needs to change.

1. my family climbed aboard the boat.

2. We sailed into the Sunset.

3. My sister, simone, sat with the captain.

4. His name was mr. Chang.

5. We All had fun.

Each sentence has an incorrect or missing punctuation mark. Circle the mistake and write the correct punctuation mark.

6. What time did the boat leave. ___

7. We will be back when it is dark ___

8. Mom and I sat up front? ___

9. It was outstanding ___

10. Can we go again ___

Each sentence has one misspelled word. Circle the misspelled word. Then, spell it correctly.

11. The wind pushed the bot through the water. _____

12. We ate dinner on tha boat. _____

Proofreading

Reading your sentences to check for mistakes is called **proofreading**. Check for mistakes in spelling, capital letters, and punctuation marks.

Proofread each sentence. Look for mistakes with capital letters and punctuation marks. Circle each mistake.

1. I'm glad for our Friendship.

2. My grandfather worked on the railroad?

3. Is bob going to pick strawberries

4. please put a stamp on the letter

5. i live on hudson street.

6. Our Neighborhood is quiet.

Each sentence has one misspelled word. Circle the misspelled word. Then, spell it correctly.

7. I will slep well tonight. _____

8. The apple tasted gud. _____

Write each sentence correctly.

9. what time is it

_____

10. sue lives in orlando, florida

_____

Proofreading

Reading your sentences to check for mistakes is called **proofreading**. Check for mistakes in spelling, capital letters, and punctuation marks.

Proofread each sentence. Look for mistakes with capital letters and punctuation marks. Circle each mistake.

1. raindrops keep falling on my head?

2. watch out.

3. My friend josie was in the crowd.

4. what is that character's name?

5. Can you sing the alphabet

6. The book is called Tale Of A Firefly.

Each sentence has one misspelled word. Circle the misspelled word. Then, spell it correctly.

7. How old ar you? _____

8. I like my teecher. _____

Write each sentence correctly.

9. which season is it

_____

10. ill see you on monday

_____

Letters

Letters have five parts: **date, greeting, body, closing,** and **name**.
  Example:
  Date: March 30, 2010

  Greeting: Dear Alice,
  Body: Thank you for the cookies. They were excellent.

  Closing: Your friend,
  Name: Dan

Label each part of the letter.

_____   June 3, 2010

_____   Dear Milli,

_____   I can come to your birthday party. See you there!

_____   Thanks,

_____   Steve

Write your own letter. Fill in the missing parts.

_____, 2009

Dear _____,

_____

_____

Your friend,

_____

Letters

Letters have five parts: **date, greeting, body, closing,** and **name**.

Label each part of the letter.

_____   April 19, 2010

_____   Dear Yasmin,

_____   I can't wait to see you next week. Have a good trip. I'll see you soon.

_____   Best wishes,

_____   Donny

Write your own letter. Fill in the missing parts.

_____, 2009

Dear _____,

_____

_____

_____,

_____

Letters

Letters have five parts: **date**, **greeting**, **body**, **closing**, and **name**.

Write two letters of your own.

Letter #1

Date _____, _____

Greeting _____,

Body _____

_____

Closing _____,

Name _____

Letter #2

_____, _____

_____,

_____

_____

_____,

_____

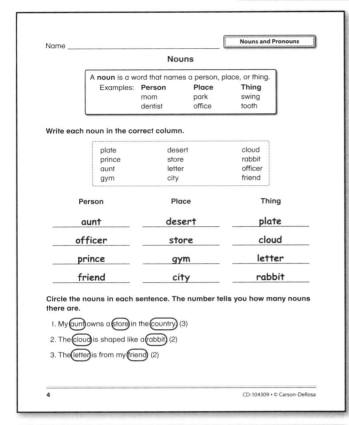

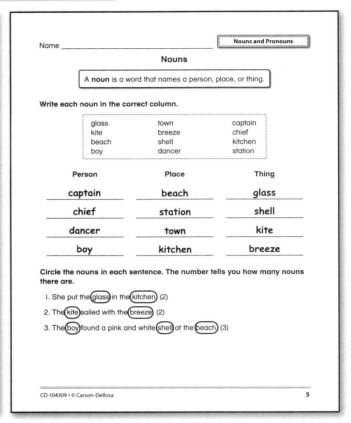

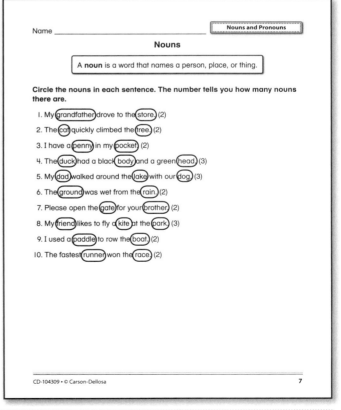

Name _____   Nouns and Pronouns

Nouns

A **noun** is a word that names a person, place, or thing.

Circle each noun in the word box below. Some words will not be circled.

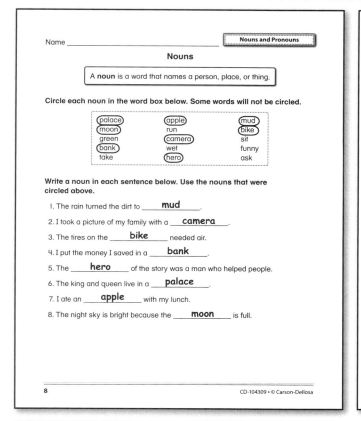

Write a noun in each sentence below. Use the nouns that were circled above.

1. The rain turned the dirt to ___mud___.

2. I took a picture of my family with a ___camera___.

3. The tires on the ___bike___ needed air.

4. I put the money I saved in a ___bank___.

5. The ___hero___ of the story was a man who helped people.

6. The king and queen live in a ___palace___.

7. I ate an ___apple___ with my lunch.

8. The night sky is bright because the ___moon___ is full.

8   CD-104309 • © Carson-Dellosa

Name _____   Nouns and Pronouns

Nouns

A **noun** is a word that names a person, place, or thing.

Circle each noun in the word box below. Some words will not be circled.

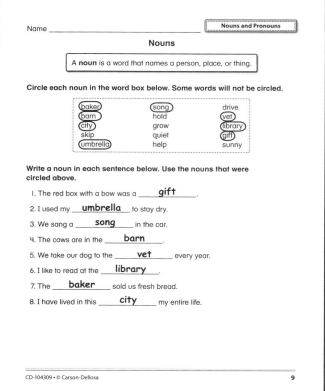

Write a noun in each sentence below. Use the nouns that were circled above.

1. The red box with a bow was a ___gift___.

2. I used my ___umbrella___ to stay dry.

3. We sang a ___song___ in the car.

4. The cows are in the ___barn___.

5. We take our dog to the ___vet___ every year.

6. I like to read at the ___library___.

7. The ___baker___ sold us fresh bread.

8. I have lived in this ___city___ my entire life.

CD-104309 • © Carson-Dellosa   9

Name _____   Nouns and Pronouns

Proper Nouns

A **proper noun** names a specific person, place, or thing. Proper nouns begin with a capital letter.

Names given to people and pets are proper nouns.
    Example: I have a hamster named *Zeke*.

Use capital letters to write the name of each person correctly.

1. cindy lewis   ___Cindy Lewis___

2. parker jones   ___Parker Jones___

3. ms. cohen   ___Ms. Cohen___

4. dan li   ___Dan Li___

5. mr. finley   ___Mr. Finley___

6. ellen garza   ___Ellen Garza___

Underline the proper noun in each sentence.

7. My cat <u>Fifi</u> likes to sleep all day.

8. <u>Julie</u> is my best friend.

9. I share a computer with <u>Angelo</u>.

10. I made a bed for my dog <u>Spot</u>.

10   CD-104309 • © Carson-Dellosa

Name _____   Nouns and Pronouns

Proper Nouns

A **proper noun** names a specific person, place, or thing. Proper nouns begin with a capital letter.

Names of places are proper nouns.
    Example: My aunt lives in *New York City*.

Use capital letters to write the name of each place correctly.

1. the corner store   ___The Corner Store___

2. miller park   ___Miller Park___

3. jameston airport   ___Jameston Airport___

4. mexico   ___Mexico___

5. first stop shop   ___First Stop Shop___

6. los angeles, california   ___Los Angeles, California___

Underline the proper noun in each sentence.

7. I like to visit <u>Jefferson Library</u>.

8. <u>Woodland School</u> is where I will go next year.

9. My grandma lives in <u>Paris, France</u>.

10. <u>Roberto's</u> is my favorite place to eat.

CD-104309 • © Carson-Dellosa   11

Worksheet (page 12)

Name _____

Proper Nouns

A **proper noun** names a specific person, place, or thing. Proper nouns begin with a capital letter.

Names of specific things, such as days of the week, months, holidays, and titles, are proper nouns.

Example: *Labor Day* is always the first *Monday* in *September*.

Use capital letters to write the name of each thing correctly.

1. the animal book — The Animal Book
2. tuesday — Tuesday
3. friday — Friday
4. june — June
5. the daily news — The Daily News
6. canada day — Canada Day

Underline the proper noun in each sentence.

7. My family is going to my uncle's house for Independence Day.
8. Have you read *Rhonda Goes Bananas*?
9. Tomorrow is Monday.
10. My birthday is in November.

12   CD-104309 • © Carson-Dellosa

Worksheet (page 13)

Name _____

Proper Nouns

A **proper noun** names a specific person, place, or thing. Proper nouns begin with a capital letter.

Write each noun and proper noun in the correct column.

| Thursday | April | ticket | Mexico City | Ms. Sho |
| farmer | teacher | park | Sunny Market | man |

Noun	Proper Noun
ticket	Thursday
teacher	April
farmer	Mexico City
park	Sunny Market
man	Ms. Sho

Circle the noun in each sentence. Underline the proper noun.

1. October is my favorite (month).
2. The (test) will be on Tuesday.
3. You can hear a (pin) drop in Townsend Library.
4. I am reading a (book) called *The Whole Story*.
5. I hugged my (mom) on Mother's Day.
6. Beanie is a small (dog).

CD-104309 • © Carson-Dellosa   13

Worksheet (page 14)

Name _____

Proper Nouns

A **proper noun** names a specific person, place, or thing. Proper nouns begin with a capital letter.

Write a proper noun to complete each sentence. Begin each proper noun with a capital letter.

Answers will vary.

People and Pets

1. My name is _____.
2. My teacher's name is _____.
3. I like spending time with my friend _____.
4. A good name for a bird is _____.

Places

5. I live in the state of _____.
6. The name of my school is _____.
7. My favorite place to eat is _____.
8. A place I would like to visit is _____.

Days, Months, Holidays, and Titles

9. My favorite day of the week is _____.
10. I like the weather in the month of _____.
11. A holiday my family takes part in is _____.
12. The next book I want to read is _____.

14   CD-104309 • © Carson-Dellosa

Worksheet (page 15)

Name _____

Plural Nouns

A **singular noun** names one person, place, or thing.
Example: Lila bought one *ticket*.

A **plural noun** names more than one person, place, or thing. You can make most nouns plural by adding the letter *s*.
Example: Lila bought two *tickets*.

Write each noun in the correct column.

| peanut | toes | crickets | guitar | swing |
| band | shirts | letters | keys | pond |

Singular	Plural
peanut	toes
guitar	crickets
swing	shirts
band	letters
pond	keys

Circle the correct word to finish each sentence.

1. Andrea fed each elephant one ((peanut)/peanuts).
2. There were three (guitar/(guitars)) at the store.
3. All of the (swing/(swings)) in the park were full.
4. Mark likes to swim in a ((pond)/ponds) in the summer.

CD-104309 • © Carson-Dellosa   15

Page 16

Name _____

Nouns and Pronouns

Plural Nouns

A **plural noun** names more than one person, place, or thing. You can make most nouns plural by adding the letter *s*.
Examples: cloud → clouds
school → schools
sister → sisters

Write each plural noun in the correct column.

birds	offices	balloons	farms
sons	dinners	kids	bakers
parks	kites	uncles	hospitals

People	Places	Things
sons	farms	birds
kids	parks	balloons
bakers	offices	dinners
uncles	hospitals	kites

Write the plural form of the noun at the end of each sentence.

1. The kitchen has two __windows__. (window)
2. Cara's party is in five __days__. (day)
3. The field is full of beautiful __flowers__. (flower)
4. Ling likes to draw __shapes__. (shape)

16   CD-104309 • © Carson-Dellosa

Page 17

Name _____

Nouns and Pronouns

Plural Nouns

A **plural noun** names more than one person, place, or thing. Nouns that end in *x*, *s*, *ch*, or *sh* become plural by adding *es*.
Examples: beach → beaches
ax → axes
dish → dishes
glass → glasses

Write the plural form of the noun at the end of each sentence.

1. I signed up for dance __classes__. (class)
2. Dad put his tools in two __boxes__. (box)
3. Maria enjoys eating __peaches__. (peach)
4. I gave my grandma good luck __wishes__. (wish)
5. The spot on the shirt came out after three __washes__. (wash)
6. Carlos saw four __foxes__. (fox)
7. He grew one and a half __inches__. (inch)
8. She bought two __dresses__. (dress)
9. I'll give you three __guesses__. (guess)
10. Glen helped clean the __brushes__. (brush)

CD-104309 • © Carson-Dellosa   17

Page 18

Name _____

Nouns and Pronouns

Plural Nouns

A **plural noun** names more than one person, place, or thing. You can make most nouns plural by adding the letter *s*. Nouns that end in *x*, *s*, *ch*, or *sh* become plural by adding *es*.

Write each noun in the correct column.

| bush | batch | pencil | bead |
| mix | light | toss | tiger |

Add *s* to Make Plural	Add *es* to Make Plural
pencil	bush
bead	batch
light	mix
tiger	toss

Circle the correct word to finish each sentence.

1. Jim cheered for two (boats/boates) in the race.
2. Lisa made a plate of (sandwichs/sandwiches) for the party.
3. I like playing (games/gamees) with friends.
4. Dad (pushs/pushes) the baby's stroller around the park.

18   CD-104309 • © Carson-Dellosa

Page 19

Name _____

Nouns and Pronouns

Plural Nouns

A **plural noun** names more than one person, place, or thing. You can make most nouns plural by adding the letter *s*. Nouns that end in *x*, *s*, *ch*, or *sh* become plural by adding *es*.

Write the plural form of each noun.

1. queen __queens__
2. fork __forks__
3. floss __flosses__
4. monkey __monkeys__
5. branch __branches__
6. ear __ears__
7. speech __speeches__
8. fix __fixes__
9. ring __rings__
10. nail __nails__

Write the plural form of the noun in each sentence.

11. The birds in the __trees__ sang. (tree)
12. Frieda liked to help her uncle cook __eggs__. (egg)
13. Peter gave two __hints__ about the gift. (hint)
14. Everyone sat on their __porches__ in the summer. (porch)
15. Many __pears__ have fallen from the tree. (pear)
16. I drank two __glasses__ of water. (glass)

CD-104309 • © Carson-Dellosa   19

Worksheet 1 (page 20)

Name _____

Plural Nouns

A **plural noun** names more than one person, place, or thing.
You can make most nouns plural by adding the letter *s*.
Nouns that end in *x, s, ch,* or *sh* become plural by adding *es*.

Solve each riddle.

1. I am made of paper, and I have two covers.

    I am a ___**book**___ .

    My plural form is ___**books**___ .

2. I am a round, fuzzy, and sweet fruit.

    I am a ___**peach**___ .

    My plural form is ___**peaches**___ .

3. I can be made of sticks and grass, and birds live in me.

    I am a ___**nest**___ .

    My plural form is ___**nests**___ .

4. I am smooth, silver, and good for eating soup.

    I am a ___**spoon**___ .

    My plural form is ___**spoons**___ .

5. I am made of sand and am next to the ocean.

    I am a ___**beach**___ .

    My plural form is ___**beaches**___ .

20   CD-104309 • © Carson-Dellosa

Worksheet 2 (page 21)

Name _____

Nouns Review

Solve each riddle with a noun from the word box below.

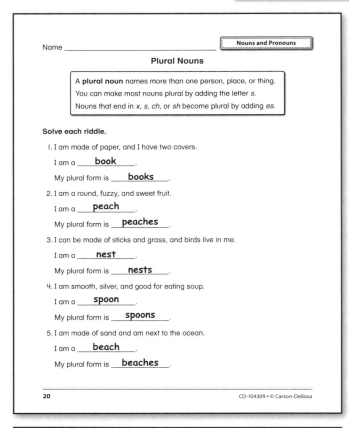

cloud	teacher	brother
zoo	hospital	vet
library	fish	baker
school	letter	kite

People

1. I help students learn. ___**teacher**___
2. I am a boy in your family. ___**brother**___
3. I make bread and sweets. ___**baker**___
4. I help animals stay well. ___**vet**___

Places

5. Students come here to learn. ___**school**___
6. Sick people come here for special care. ___**hospital**___
7. People come here to look at animals. ___**zoo**___
8. There are many shelves of books here. ___**library**___

Things

9. I look white and fluffy. ___**cloud**___
10. I live in water. ___**fish**___
11. I am used to spell words. ___**letter**___
12. I fly in the sky on windy days. ___**kite**___

CD-104309 • © Carson-Dellosa   21

Worksheet 3 (page 22)

Name _____

Nouns Review

lizard	minute	lunches	leaf
Father's Day	guards	campfire	The South Market
Monday	foxes	Ms. March	oceans

Write a singular noun from the word box to finish each sentence.

1. The game will begin in one ___**minute**___ .
2. I watched the ___**lizard**___ crawl up the tree.
3. A red ___**leaf**___ floated down from the tree.
4. Bob and Janell sang around the ___**campfire**___ for hours.

Write a plural noun from the word box to finish each sentence.

5. Seven ___**guards**___ stood in front of the palace.
6. Gail has flown in an airplane over two ___**oceans**___ .
7. James ate an apple at three ___**lunches**___ in a row.
8. I saw two ___**foxes**___ running into the forest.

Write a proper noun from the word box to finish each sentence.

9. My dad will be surprised on ___**Father's Day**___ .
10. I called ___**Ms. March**___ to tell her I would be late.
11. Mom and I shop at ___**The South Market**___ on Saturdays.
12. My favorite day is ___**Monday**___ .

22   CD-104309 • © Carson-Dellosa

Worksheet 4 (page 23)

Name _____

Nouns Review

market	day	The Big Adventure	doctors
flutes	dishes	Green Park	Toto
Columbus Day	holidays	spoon	snack

Write a singular noun from the word box to finish each sentence.

1. My dad makes me a ___**snack**___ after school.
2. I hold my ___**spoon**___ with my left hand.
3. This is the ___**day**___ I have been waiting for.
4. Grace is going to the ___**market**___ to get fruit.

Write a plural noun from the word box to finish each sentence.

5. My job is to wash the ___**dishes**___ after dinner.
6. There are eight ___**flutes**___ in the band.
7. Philip spends most ___**holidays**___ with his aunt and uncle.
8. Both ___**doctors**___ said I had the flu.

Write a proper noun from the word box to finish each sentence.

9. I am reading a book called ___**The Big Adventure**___ .
10. Mr. Lewis likes to walk at ___**Green Park**___ .
11. Shanda named her dog ___**Toto**___ .
12. School is out for ___**Columbus Day**___ .

CD-104309 • © Carson-Dellosa   23

Page 24

Name _____

Pronouns

A **pronoun** is a word that can take the place of a noun. *I, me, we, us, you, he, him, she, her, it, they,* and *them* are examples of pronouns.
Examples: Anna likes to run. → *She* likes to run.
Bobby enjoys soccer. → *He* enjoys soccer.

Write *he, she, it, we,* or *they* in place of the underlined words.

1. My sister and I need to water the plants.
   We need to water the plants.

2. The sunset was colorful.
   It was colorful.

3. Derek is happy because it is Monday.
   He is happy because it is Monday.

4. Emma and Drew watched the peacock.
   They watched the peacock.

5. Aunt Karen asked her friends to lunch.
   She asked her friends to lunch.

6. My brothers play fun games.
   They play fun games.

7. The red wagon has a flat tire.
   It has a flat tire.

8. My friends and I are in the same class.
   We are in the same class.

24   CD-104309 • © Carson-Dellosa

Page 25

Name _____

Pronouns

A **pronoun** is a word that can take the place of a noun. *I, me, we, us, you, he, him, she, her, it, they,* and *them* are examples of pronouns.

Write *he, she, it, we,* or *they* in place of the underlined words.

1. The computer was a gift to the school.
   It was a gift to the school.

2. The Johnsons moved into the house next door.
   They moved into the house next door.

3. My dad likes to cook on the weekends.
   He likes to cook on the weekends.

4. Clara Barton was a nurse.
   She was a nurse.

5. Good friends are important.
   They are important.

6. Chris and I are going camping with my family.
   We are going camping with my family.

Write a sentence using each pronoun. **Answers will vary.**

7. (I) _____

8. (You) _____

9. (We) _____

10. (They) _____

CD-104309 • © Carson-Dellosa   25

Page 26

Name _____

Pronouns

A **pronoun** is a word that can take the place of a noun. *I, me, we, us, you, he, him, she, her, it, they,* and *them* are examples of pronouns.
Examples: Ann smiled at Lisa. → Ann smiled at *her.*
Celia won the race. → Celia won *it.*

Write *him, her, it, us,* or *them* in place of the underlined words.

1. Heidi wants to surprise Javier.
   Heidi wants to surprise **him**.

2. Mom asked Grandma to stay at our house.
   Mom asked **her** to stay at our house.

3. The tickets are for Dayton and me.
   The tickets are for **us**.

4. Please save seats for Aisha and Lynn.
   Please save seats for **them**.

5. I am going to the park with Uncle Jim.
   I am going to the park with **him**.

6. Did you hear about the new bridge?
   Did you hear about **it**?

7. Marla needs to fix her bike before Friday.
   Marla needs to fix **it** before Friday.

8. Dad is spending the day with my friends and me.
   Dad is spending the day with **us**.

26   CD-104309 • © Carson-Dellosa

Page 27

Name _____

Pronouns

A **pronoun** is a word that can take the place of a noun. *I, me, we, us, you, he, him, she, her, it, they,* and *them* are examples of pronouns.

Write *him, her, it, us,* or *them* in place of the underlined words.

1. I can hear your voice from the back row.
   I can hear **it** from the back row.

2. What would you like Anna and Bob to do?
   What would you like **them** to do?

3. Marty took a picture of Sarah and me.
   Marty took a picture of **us**.

4. Jacob handed the phone to me.
   Jacob handed **it** to me.

5. I made a necklace for my stepmom.
   I made a necklace for **her**.

6. This shirt is for Larry.
   This shirt is for **him**.

Write a sentence using each pronoun. **Answers will vary.**

7. (me) _____

8. (you) _____

9. (us) _____

10. (them) _____

CD-104309 • © Carson-Dellosa   27

Page 28

Name _____

Verbs

Verbs

A **verb** is a word that shows action. Some verbs tell what is happening now. These verbs are called **present tense verbs**.
Examples: run   I *run* on the playground.
walk   Donna and Winston *walk* to school.
play   We *play* together.

Write the correct verb to finish each group of words.

| swim | catch | win | read | eat | drive |

1. **eat** the food
2. **swim** in the pool
3. **drive** the car
4. **catch** the ball
5. **win** the race
6. **read** the book

Write the correct verb to finish each sentence.

| sleeps | works | rides | listens | spills | finds |

7. My mom **listens** to the radio in the morning.
8. Susan **works** at a store near her house.
9. Uncle Bill **rides** the bus to work.
10. José **sleeps** later on the weekends.
11. Lily **spills** her juice when she is in a hurry.
12. Dad **finds** pennies every place we go!

28   CD-104309 • © Carson-Dellosa

Page 29

Name _____

Verbs

Verbs

A **verb** is a word that shows action. Some verbs tell what is happening now. These verbs are called **present tense verbs**.

Write the correct verb to finish each group of words.

| smile | bake | plant | shop | dig | dive |

1. **dive** into the pool
2. **bake** a cake
3. **smile** at my friend
4. **shop** at the market
5. **dig** a hole
6. **plant** a tree

Write the correct verb to finish each sentence.

| bloom | build | march | carry | sail | sing |

7. Flowers **bloom** in the spring.
8. Robert and Heather **sail** a boat on the lake.
9. My friends **march** in the parade each year.
10. Ants **carry** food to their nest.
11. Birds **build** their nests in trees.
12. He and I **sing** together in the choir.

CD-104309 • © Carson-Dellosa   29

Page 30

Name _____

Verbs

Verbs

A **verb** is a word that shows action. Some verbs tell what is happening now. These verbs are called **present tense verbs**.

Circle the verb in each sentence.

1. My dog Toto (runs) fast.
2. Erin (thinks) about the question.
3. He (goes) to class.
4. We (paint) pictures of flowers.
5. They (climb) to the top of the mountain.
6. Jim (plays) his guitar at lunch.
7. Henry (builds) snowmen during winter.
8. Hailey and I (go) to camp together.
9. Marie (watches) the parade from her window.
10. White clouds (float) in the blue sky.
11. The artist (paints) beautiful pictures.
12. He (opens) his eyes.

30   CD-104309 • © Carson-Dellosa

Page 31

Name _____

Verbs

Past Tense Verbs

A **verb** is a word that can tell what is happening now or what has already happened. Verbs that tell what is happening now are **present tense verbs**. Verbs that tell what has already happened are **past tense verbs**.

Many verbs add *ed* to show the past tense.
Examples: PRESENT   walk   I *walk* to school.
PAST   walked I *walked* to school.

Write the past tense of each verb.

1. mow   **mowed**
2. climb   **climbed**
3. boil   **boiled**
4. open   **opened**
5. push   **pushed**
6. fill   **filled**

Write the past tense of each verb to finish the story.

When I **visited** Aunt Peggy last summer, we had fun. Each morning, we
(visit)
mixed cereal and berries together for breakfast. We **pulled**
(mix)   (pull)
chairs onto her back porch and **talked** until it was time for lunch!
(talk)
At lunch, we **picked** lettuce from her garden for a salad. After lunch,
(pick)
we **planted** flowers. Then, we **watched** movies at night.
(plant)   (watch)
I **asked** Aunt Peggy if I could come back this summer!
(ask)

CD-104309 • © Carson-Dellosa   31

Name _____   Verbs

Past Tense Verbs

A **verb** is a word that can tell what is happening now or what has already happened. Verbs that tell what is happening now are **present tense verbs**. Verbs that tell what has already happened are **past tense verbs**.

Many verbs add *ed* to show the past tense.
Examples: PRESENT cheer   Darrell and Hunter *cheer* at the game.
          PAST   cheered Darrell and Hunter *cheered* at the game.

Write the past tense of each verb.

1. trust **trusted**   4. turn **turned**
2. work   **worked**   5. lock **locked**
3. count **counted**   6. rest **rested**

Write the correct past tense verb to finish each group of words.

| carried | cooked | jumped | shopped | stopped | raced |

7. **jumped** over the puddle
8. **carried** my books
9. **stopped** at the stop sign
10. **shopped** at the market
11. **cooked** dinner
12. **raced** around the track

Name _____   Verbs

Past Tense Verbs

A **verb** is a word that can tell what is happening now or what has already happened. Verbs that tell what is happening now are **present tense verbs**. Verbs that tell what has already happened are **past tense verbs**.

Many verbs add *ed* to show the past tense.
Examples: PRESENT play   Ana and Erica *play* at recess.
          PAST   played Ana and Erica *played* at recess.

Circle the past tense verb to finish each sentence.

1. We (pick/**picked**) strawberries this morning.
2. I (smile/**smiled**) when I got my test back.
3. Mary (search/**searched**) for her pencil.
4. Grandma (mend/**mended**) the tear in my shirt.
5. We (mix/**mixed**) oil and vinegar to put on the salad.

Write the correct past tense verb to finish each sentence.

| listened | rolled | followed | hopped | whispered |

6. We **listened** to the dog bark for hours.
7. Susan **rolled** the yarn into a ball.
8. Sam **hopped** like a kangaroo.
9. Melissa **whispered** a secret in my ear.
10. Isaac **followed** the sweet smell to the bakery.

Name _____   Verbs

Past Tense Verbs

A **verb** is a word that can tell what is happening now or what has already happened. Verbs that tell what is happening now are **present tense verbs**. Verbs that tell what has already happened are **past tense verbs**.

Many verbs add *ed* to show the past tense.
Examples: PRESENT wash   Andrea and Walt *wash* the car.
          PAST   washed Andrea and Walt *washed* the car.

Circle the past tense verb to finish each sentence.

1. My stepdad (stir/**stirred**) the soup.
2. I (watch/**watched**) the sun set yesterday.
3. Lynn (tie/**tied**) a bow on the gift.
4. My brother and I (serve/**served**) dinner to our mom yesterday.
5. Julie (lock/**locked**) the door behind her.

Write the past tense of each verb to finish the story.

Last weekend, I **played** in a soccer game. The game **started** early,
(play)   (start)
but it **finished** late. Both teams **wanted** to win. The score
    (finish)   (want)
stayed tied for almost the whole game. Our team **pushed** ahead and
(stay)   (push)
never **rested** . I think we **surprised** the other team! In the end, we
      (rest)   (surprise)
kicked the winning goal. The crowd **roared** .
(kick)   (roar)

Name _____   Verbs

Past Tense Irregular Verbs

Some verbs use a different form of the same word to tell the past tense. These are called **irregular verbs**.
Examples: PRESENT eat We *eat* lunch at noon.
          PAST   ate We *ate* lunch at noon.

Draw a line to match each verb with the correct past tense form.

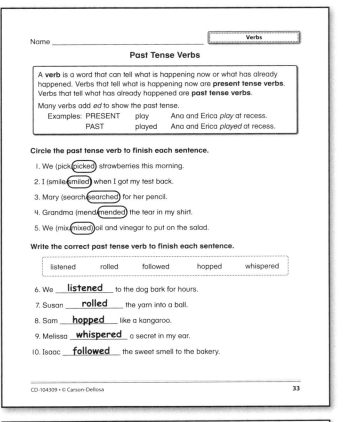

1. sleep   gave
2. hold   fell
3. make   left
4. win   bought
5. give   held
6. fall   made
7. buy   won
8. drink   drank
9. ride   slept
10. leave   rode

Write the past tense of each irregular verb to finish the sentence.

11. Lori **made** a card for Samantha.
    (make)
12. Lindsey **held** her cat at the vet.
    (hold)
13. She **bought** enough bread for a week.
    (buy)
14. Our team **won** the game!
    (win)

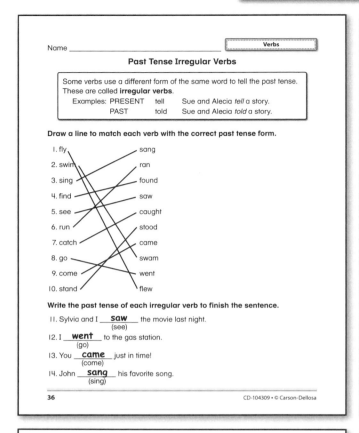

Name _____ Verbs

Past Tense Irregular Verbs

Some verbs use a different form of the same word to tell the past tense. These are called **irregular verbs**.

Examples: PRESENT   tell   Sue and Alecia *tell* a story.
PAST   told   Sue and Alecia *told* a story.

Draw a line to match each verb with the correct past tense form.

1. fly
2. swim
3. sing
4. find
5. see
6. run
7. catch
8. go
9. come
10. stand

sang
ran
found
saw
caught
stood
came
swam
went
flew

Write the past tense of each irregular verb to finish the sentence.

11. Sylvia and I __**saw**__ the movie last night.
   (see)
12. I __**went**__ to the gas station.
   (go)
13. You __**came**__ just in time!
   (come)
14. John __**sang**__ his favorite song.
   (sing)

36   CD-104309 • © Carson-Dellosa

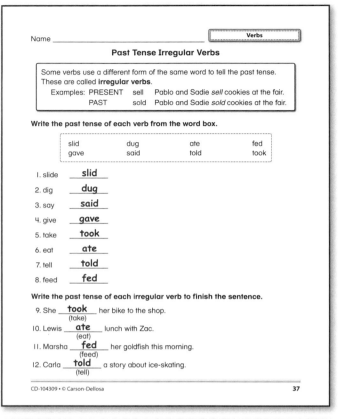

Name _____ Verbs

Past Tense Irregular Verbs

Some verbs use a different form of the same word to tell the past tense. These are called **irregular verbs**.

Examples: PRESENT   sell   Pablo and Sadie *sell* cookies at the fair.
PAST   sold   Pablo and Sadie *sold* cookies at the fair.

Write the past tense of each verb from the word box.

| slid | dug | ate | fed |
| gave | said | told | took |

1. slide __**slid**__
2. dig __**dug**__
3. say __**said**__
4. give __**gave**__
5. take __**took**__
6. eat __**ate**__
7. tell __**told**__
8. feed __**fed**__

Write the past tense of each irregular verb to finish the sentence.

9. She __**took**__ her bike to the shop.
   (take)
10. Lewis __**ate**__ lunch with Zac.
   (eat)
11. Marsha __**fed**__ her goldfish this morning.
   (feed)
12. Carla __**told**__ a story about ice-skating.
   (tell)

CD-104309 • © Carson-Dellosa   37

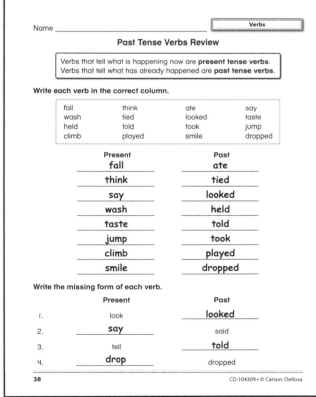

Name _____ Verbs

Past Tense Verbs Review

Verbs that tell what is happening now are **present tense verbs**.
Verbs that tell what has already happened are **past tense verbs**.

Write each verb in the correct column.

fall	think	ate	say
wash	tied	looked	taste
held	told	took	jump
climb	played	smile	dropped

Present	Past
fall	**ate**
think	**tied**
say	**looked**
wash	**held**
taste	**told**
jump	**took**
climb	**played**
smile	**dropped**

Write the missing form of each verb.

	Present	Past
1.	look	**looked**
2.	**say**	said
3.	tell	**told**
4.	**drop**	dropped

38   CD-104309 • © Carson-Dellosa

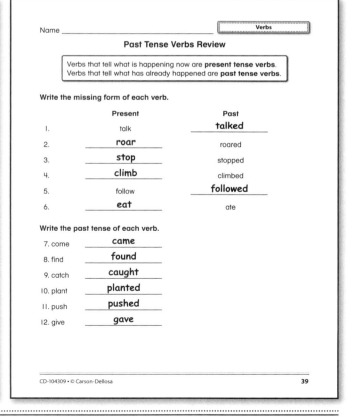

Name _____ Verbs

Past Tense Verbs Review

Verbs that tell what is happening now are **present tense verbs**.
Verbs that tell what has already happened are **past tense verbs**.

Write the missing form of each verb.

	Present	Past
1.	talk	**talked**
2.	**roar**	roared
3.	**stop**	stopped
4.	**climb**	climbed
5.	follow	**followed**
6.	**eat**	ate

Write the past tense of each verb.

7. come __**came**__
8. find __**found**__
9. catch __**caught**__
10. plant __**planted**__
11. push __**pushed**__
12. give __**gave**__

CD-104309 • © Carson-Dellosa   39

Name _____

Verbs

State-of-Being Verbs: *Am*, *Is*, and *Are*

State-of-being verbs do not show action. They tell about something that exists now or that existed in the past. *Am, is,* and *are* are examples of state-of-being verbs that tell that something exists now.

Use *am* after the word *I.*
   Example: I *am* hungry.

Use *is* to tell about one noun or pronoun.
   Examples: This *is* my shirt. Today *is* Monday.

Use *are* after the word *you* or with plural nouns and pronouns.
   Examples: You *are* a teacher. Dolphins *are* animals.

Write *am, is,* or *are* to complete each sentence.

1. My hamster **is** light brown.
2. I **am** the tallest girl on the team.
3. My lunch **is** in my backpack.
4. You **are** in line for the water fountain.
5. I **am** ready to go swimming.
6. Jonah's friends **are** laughing at a joke.
7. This candy **is** too sweet!
8. Aunt Pat **is** listening to violin music.
9. We **are** painting my room purple.
10. I **am** the president of the student council.

40

CD-104309 • © Carson-Dellosa

Name _____

Verbs

State-of-Being Verbs: *Am*, *Is*, and *Are*

State-of-being verbs do not show action. They tell about something that exists now or that existed in the past. *Am, is,* and *are* are examples of state-of-being verbs that tell that something exists now.

Write *am, is,* or *are* to complete each sentence.

1. The moon **is** bright tonight.
2. That car **is** my granddad's.
3. I **am** hungry.
4. You **are** the first person I met.
5. The trees **are** bent from the storm.
6. Seven ladybugs **are** on the window.
7. She **is** building a dollhouse.
8. Jordin **is** on time every day.

Write a sentence with the word *am*.

9. **Answers will vary.** _____

Write a sentence with the word *is*.

10. **Answers will vary.** _____

Write a sentence with the word *are*.

11. **Answers will vary.** _____

CD-104309 • © Carson-Dellosa

41

Name _____

Verbs

State-of-Being Verbs: *Was* and *Were*

State-of-being verbs do not show action. They tell about something that exists now or that existed in the past. *Was* and *were* are examples of state-of-being verbs that tell that something existed in the past.

Use *was* to tell about one person, place, or thing.
   Example: I *was* hungry.

Use *were* with *you* or with more than one person, place, or thing.
   Examples: You *were* at the party. Sara and Bob *were* glad.

Write *was* or *were* to complete each sentence.

1. My window **was** open all night.
2. I **was** surprised on my birthday this year.
3. You **were** running to the library.
4. Eli **was** at the play last night.
5. Mom and Dad **were** sitting in the front row.
6. You **were** the winner!
7. They **were** able to see the ocean.
8. Jorge **was** trying to catch a fly.
9. The evening light **was** soft.
10. The clothes **were** on sale.

42

CD-104309 • © Carson-Dellosa

Name _____

Verbs

State-of-Being Verbs: *Was* and *Were*

State-of-being verbs do not show action. They tell about something that exists now or that existed in the past. *Was* and *were* are examples of state-of-being verbs that tell that something existed in the past.

Write *was* or *were* to complete each sentence.

1. Breakfast **was** wonderful!
2. You **were** out of town.
3. Paul **was** on the bus.
4. I **was** looking the other way.
5. The movie **was** good.
6. All the monkeys **were** in one tree.
7. Ms. Mui **was** gone for a week.
8. You and I **were** on the same team.

Write a sentence with the word *was*.

9. **Answers will vary.** _____

Write a sentence with the word *were*.

10. **Answers will vary.** _____

CD-104309 • © Carson-Dellosa

43

Name _____ **Verbs**

Verbs: *Has* and *Have*

> Some **verbs** do not show action. They tell about something that exists now or that existed in the past. *Has* and *have* are examples of verbs that tell that something exists now.
>
> Use *has* to tell about one person, place, or thing.
>> Example: She *has* blue eyes.
>
> Use *have* with *you* and *I* and with more than one person, place, or thing.
>> Examples: I *have* brown hair.
>> You *have* red hair.
>> Dan and Sue *have* black hair.

Write *has* or *have* to complete each sentence.

1. Sharon's apartment __has__ lots of windows.
2. I __have__ a dog and two cats.
3. You __have__ beautiful eyes.
4. Jackie __has__ many books.
5. The table __has__ three legs.
6. Some houses __have__ fences.
7. He __has__ two sisters.
8. The cats __have__ many toys.
9. Each day __has__ its surprises.
10. Kelly and Mac __have__ a red wagon.

Name _____ **Verbs**

Verbs: *Has* and *Have*

> Some **verbs** do not show action. They tell about something that exists now or that existed in the past. *Has* and *have* are examples of verbs that tell that something exists now.

Write *has* or *have* to complete each sentence.

1. We __have__ fun plans for this summer.
2. The school __has__ Friday off.
3. My dad __has__ three fishing poles.
4. The girl __has__ a hat.
5. Lia and I __have__ tomatoes on our sandwiches.
6. The doghouses __have__ new roofs.
7. His sister __has__ dance shoes.
8. The zoo __has__ many animals.

Write a sentence with the word *has*.

9. __Answers will vary.__

Write a sentence with the word *have*.

10. __Answers will vary.__

Name _____ **Verbs**

Verbs Review

> A **verb** shows an action or a state of being.

All of the words below are verbs. Circle the verbs that you have done already today. Underline the verbs that you think you will do later today.

wake	brush	eat	bake	use
laugh	hold	give	stand	jump
sit	think	talk	walk	sing
paint	climb	study	read	rest
ride	smile	skate	feed	build
play	wish	sleep	wave	swing

Write three more verbs you will do today.   **Answers will vary.**

_____

_____

_____

Solve each riddle with a word from the word box above.

1. I am something you do to your hair and your teeth.

   What verb am I? __brush__

2. I am something you can do only with your eyes closed.

   What verb am I? __sleep__

Name _____ **Adjectives**

Adjectives

> **Adjectives** are words that describe, or tell about, nouns.
> Examples: a *good* friend   the *blue* sky
>   a *quiet* room   the *beautiful* dress

Write the best adjective to finish each group of words.

soft	bright	loud	huge	yellow	funny

1. the __funny__ clown
2. a __yellow__ school bus
3. a __bright__ light
4. the __loud__ music
5. a __huge__ elephant
6. the __soft__ pillow

Write the best adjective to finish each sentence.

low	warm	cute	busy	equal	tiny

7. I put an __equal__ amount of soup in my bowl and yours.
8. We waited to cross the __busy__ street.
9. I saw a __tiny__ bug on my desk.
10. Josie got a __cute__ puppy from the animal shelter.
11. It is a __warm__ day to wear a sweater.
12. Alice stepped over the __low__ wall.

Page 48

Name _____

Adjectives

Adjectives

> **Adjectives** are words that describe, or tell about, nouns.
> Examples: a *cute* baby   the *dry* dirt
>   a *kind* boy   the *deep* hole

Write the best adjective to complete each group of words.

| famous | smooth | shiny | narrow | cool | golden |

1. the __**golden**__ sun
2. a __**smooth**__ rock
3. a __**shiny**__ penny
4. the __**cool**__ breeze
5. a __**narrow**__ path
6. a __**famous**__ person

Circle the adjective that describes the weather today. Answers will vary.

7. Today, the weather is (warm/cool).
8. The sky is (blue/gray).
9. It is (wet/dry).
10. It is a (beautiful/cloudy) day!

48   CD-104309 • © Carson-Dellosa

Page 49

Name _____

Adjectives

Adjectives: Size and Shape

> **Adjectives** are words that describe, or tell about, nouns.
> Some adjectives describe size or shape.
> Examples: SIZE   a *small* dog   a *giant* tree
>   SHAPE   a *square* door   a *round* window

Circle the adjectives that describe size. Underline the adjectives that describe shape.

square | (long) | round | pointed | (large) | (tall)
(giant) | (tiny) | oval | (small) | (wide) | (narrow)

Write a noun that each adjective can describe.   Answers will vary.

1. a square _____
2. a long _____
3. a round _____
4. a pointed _____
5. a large _____
6. a tall _____

7. a giant _____
8. a tiny _____
9. an oval _____
10. a small _____
11. a wide _____
12. a narrow _____

CD-104309 • © Carson-Dellosa   49

Page 50

Name _____

Adjectives

Adjectives: Color and Number

> **Adjectives** are words that describe, or tell about, nouns.
> Some adjectives describe color or number.
> Examples: COLOR   a *white* fence   *blue* eyes
>   NUMBER   *one* house   *many* balloons

Circle the adjectives that describe color. Underline the adjectives that describe number.

(purple) | (green) | twenty | several | some | (black)
(gray) | eleven | two | (tan) | fifteen | few

Write an adjective that describes color.   Answers will vary.

1. I would like a _____ shirt.
2. The room has _____ walls.
3. I am wearing _____ shoes.
4. I have _____ hair.
5. I like _____ flowers.

Write an adjective that describes number.   Answers will vary.

6. I drink about _____ glasses of water each day.
7. I sleep about _____ hours each night.
8. The room I am in has _____ windows.
9. I can think of _____ ways to say hello to someone.
10. I would like _____ apple slices after school.

50   CD-104309 • © Carson-Dellosa

Page 51

Name _____

Adjectives

Adjectives: Senses

> **Adjectives** are words that describe, or tell about, nouns.
> Some adjectives describe how something looks, sounds, tastes, smells, or feels.
> Examples: LOOKS   a *pretty* horse
>   SOUNDS   a *quiet* voice
>   TASTES   a *sweet* cookie
>   FEELS   a *fuzzy* rabbit

Write each adjective in the correct column.

| salty | green | rough | sweet | loud | scary |
| quiet | dark | sour | beautiful | heavy | smooth |

Looks	Sounds	Tastes	Feels
green	loud	salty	rough
dark	quiet	sour	heavy
beautiful	scary	sweet	smooth

Write your own adjective to complete each sentence.   Answers will vary.

1. I like _____ food.
2. I like _____ music.
3. I like _____ weather.
4. I saw a _____ sunset last night.
5. I heard a _____ whistle.
6. I felt a _____ tap on my shoulder.

CD-104309 • © Carson-Dellosa   51

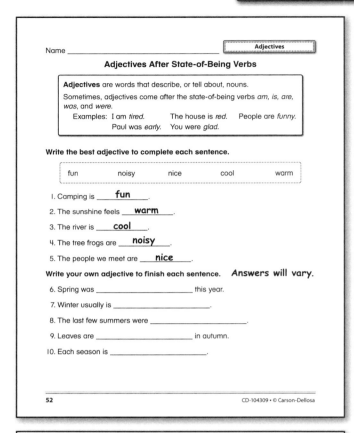

Name _____

Adjectives

Adjectives After State-of-Being Verbs

Adjectives are words that describe, or tell about, nouns.

Sometimes, adjectives come after the state-of-being verbs *am*, *is*, *are*, *was*, and *were*.

Examples: I am *tired*. The house is *red*. People are *funny*.
Paul was *early*. You were *glad*.

Write the best adjective to complete each sentence.

| fun | noisy | nice | cool | warm |

1. Camping is **fun**.
2. The sunshine feels **warm**.
3. The river is **cool**.
4. The tree frogs are **noisy**.
5. The people we meet are **nice**.

Write your own adjective to finish each sentence. **Answers will vary.**

6. Spring was _____ this year.
7. Winter usually is _____.
8. The last few summers were _____.
9. Leaves are _____ in autumn.
10. Each season is _____.

52 CD-104309 • © Carson-Dellosa

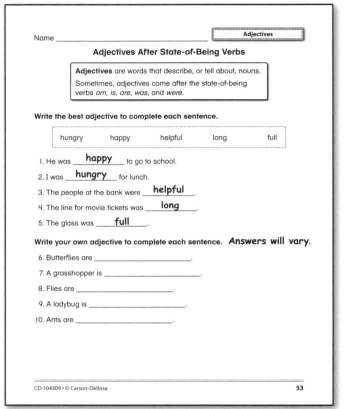

Name _____

Adjectives

Adjectives After State-of-Being Verbs

Adjectives are words that describe, or tell about, nouns.

Sometimes, adjectives come after the state-of-being verbs *am*, *is*, *are*, *was*, and *were*.

Write the best adjective to complete each sentence.

| hungry | happy | helpful | long | full |

1. He was **happy** to go to school.
2. I was **hungry** for lunch.
3. The people at the bank were **helpful**.
4. The line for movie tickets was **long**.
5. The glass was **full**.

Write your own adjective to complete each sentence. **Answers will vary.**

6. Butterflies are _____.
7. A grasshopper is _____.
8. Flies are _____.
9. A ladybug is _____.
10. Ants are _____.

CD-104309 • © Carson-Dellosa 53

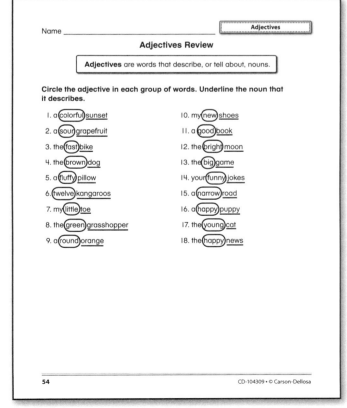

Name _____

Adjectives

Adjectives Review

Adjectives are words that describe, or tell about, nouns.

Circle the adjective in each group of words. Underline the noun that it describes.

1. a (colorful) sunset
2. a (sour) grapefruit
3. the (fast) bike
4. the (brown) dog
5. a (fluffy) pillow
6. (twelve) kangaroos
7. my (little) toe
8. the (green) grasshopper
9. a (round) orange
10. my (new) shoes
11. a (good) book
12. the (bright) moon
13. the (big) game
14. your (funny) jokes
15. a (narrow) road
16. a (happy) puppy
17. the (young) cat
18. the (happy) news

54 CD-104309 • © Carson-Dellosa

Name _____

Adjectives

Adjectives Review

Circle the adjective that describes each underlined noun.

1. I helped plant a (beautiful) garden at my school.
2. The dirt was (rocky) so we added soil.
3. We planted tomato plants in (five) rows.
4. We will pick them when they are (ripe).
5. Then, we will make a (tasty) sauce for spaghetti.

Circle two adjectives that describe each underlined noun.

6. I have a (blue) and (green) coat.
7. It is (big) and (warm).
8. My mom made the coat from (old) (colorful) sweaters.
9. It is my (special) (winter) coat.
10. I wear it (every) (cold) day.

Circle all of the adjectives in each sentence. The number tells you how many there are.

11. I am helping my dad build a (new) doghouse for Bingo. (1)
12. He asked me to bring him (four) (long) nails and (one) hammer. (3)
13. He asked me to draw a (round) shape for the door and (two) squares for windows. (2)
14. We worked all day on a (sunny) Saturday and finished. (1)
15. Bingo is (happy) and my dad and I are (tired). (2)

CD-104309 • © Carson-Dellosa 55

Name _____

Adjectives

Adjectives That Compare

You can compare two nouns by adding *er* to many adjectives. You can compare more than two nouns by adding *est* to many adjectives.
Examples: Lucy is *taller* than Lara.
Nina is the *tallest* girl in the class.

Write *er* at the end of each adjective to compare the two things in each sentence.

1. Tom's kitten is ____**older**____ than Steve's kitten.
(old)

2. February is usually ____**colder**____ than March.
(cold)

3. My pillow is ____**softer**____ than my sister's pillow.
(soft)

4. Cloudy nights are ____**darker**____ than clear nights.
(dark)

5. Mindy's dinner is ____**warmer**____ than Lupe's dinner.
(warm)

Write *est* at the end of each adjective to compare the things in each sentence.

6. Rhode Island is the ____**smallest**____ state in the United States.
(small)

7. The red car is the ____**fastest**____ on the track.
(fast)

8. This is the ____**coolest**____ weather that we have had this month.
(cool)

9. That apple is the ____**highest**____ in the tree.
(high)

10. Your smile is the ____**brightest**____ one I have seen!
(bright)

56

CD-104309 • © Carson-Dellosa

Name _____

Adjectives

Adjectives That Compare

You can compare two nouns by adding *er* to many adjectives. You can compare more than two nouns by adding *est* to many adjectives.
Examples: Autumn is *colder* than summer.
Winter is the *coldest* time of year.

Write the missing form of each word.

	Compares Two Things	Compares More Than Two Things
1.	longer	**longest**
2.	**taller**	tallest
3.	warmer	**warmest**
4.	**shorter**	shortest
5.	**faster**	fastest
6.	**higher**	highest
7.	sharper	**sharpest**
8.	cooler	**coolest**
9.	**older**	oldest
10.	younger	**youngest**

Write a sentence comparing two things.

11. **Answers will vary.** _____

Write a sentence comparing more than two things.

12. **Answers will vary.** _____

CD-104309 • © Carson-Dellosa

57

Name _____

Adjectives

Articles

A, *an*, and *the* are a special kind of adjective called **articles**. They help nouns.

A is used before a noun that begins with a consonant.
Example: *a* beetle

An is used before a noun that begins with a vowel.
Example: *an* ant

The is used before a noun that names a particular person, place, or thing.
Example: *the* bear

Write *a* or *an* for each noun.

1. __**a**__ forest
2. __**a**__ plant
3. __**an**__ umbrella
4. __**an**__ elevator
5. __**an**__ arrow

6. __**a**__ gallon
7. __**a**__ triangle
8. __**an**__ oar
9. __**an**__ idea
10. __**a**__ newspaper

Write *a*, *an*, or *the* to finish each sentence.

11. Miriam and Todd walked to __**the**__ pond.

12. They saw __**a**__ lizard running up a tree.

13. They saw a fish swimming in __**the**__ water.

14. Todd got hungry and took __**an**__ apple out of his bag.

15. Miriam ate __**a**__ banana.

58

CD-104309 • © Carson-Dellosa

Name _____

Adjectives

Articles

A, *an*, and *the* are a special kind of adjective called **articles**. They help nouns.

A is used before a noun that begins with a consonant.
Example: *a* chair

An is used before a noun that begins with a vowel.
Example: *an* egg

The is used before a noun that names a particular person, place, or thing.
Example: *the* woman

Write *a* or *an* for each noun.

1. __**a**__ zipper
2. __**an**__ owl
3. __**an**__ itch
4. __**a**__ dish
5. __**a**__ brother

6. __**a**__ clown
7. __**an**__ airplane
8. __**an**__ oven
9. __**a**__ sale
10. __**an**__ actor

Write a sentence with *a*.

11. **Answers will vary.** _____

Write a sentence with *an*.

12. **Answers will vary.** _____

Write a sentence with *the*.

13. **Answers will vary.** _____

CD-104309 • © Carson-Dellosa

59

Name _____   **Parts of Speech Review**

Parts of Speech Review

Write a word that fits each description. Answers will vary.

I. verb (past tense)

7. noun (thing, plural)

2. proper noun (title of a book)

8. adjective (number more than one)

3. adjective (sense)

9. adjective (color)

4. proper noun (name of a person)

10. noun (person)

5. noun (place)

11. adjective (after state-of-being verb)

6. verb (now)

**Write the words from the numbers above to complete the story below.
Read your story to a friend.**

A Kind Gorilla

I just (1)_____ a book called (2)_____. It was about a

(3)_____ gorilla named (4)_____. In the story, the gorilla

lives in a (5)_____. The gorilla (6)_____ all day and eats

(7)_____ off the trees. One day, the gorilla finds (8)_____

(9)_____ kittens that are lost. The gorilla helps the kittens find their

(10)_____. In the end, everyone is (11)_____.

60   CD-104309 • © Carson-Dellosa

Name _____   **Parts of Speech Review**

Parts of Speech Review

**For each sentence, write *N* if the underlined word is a noun, *V* if it is a verb,
A if it is an adjective, or *P* if it is a pronoun.**

__A__ I. Mary had a <u>little</u> lamb.

__V__ 2. The cow <u>jumped</u> over the moon.

__N__ 3. He lives on <u>Drury Lane</u>.

__V__ 4. Jack and Jill <u>went</u> up the hill.

__P__ 5. The less <u>he</u> spoke, the more he heard.

__N__ 6. An apple a day keeps the <u>doctor</u> away.

__A__ 7. The ants go marching <u>one</u> by one.

__N__ 8. How does your <u>garden</u> grow?

Circle the adjective that describes the underlined noun.

9. We sing a (quiet) song before bed.

10. My stepmom wishes me (sweet) dreams.

11. Sometimes, Dad tells (short) stories.

12. I get into my (warm) bed and go to sleep.

Write the sentence in number 9 in the past tense.

13. **We sang a quiet song before bed.**

Write the sentence in number 10 in the past tense.

14. **My stepmom wished me sweet dreams.**

Write the sentence in number 11 with a pronoun.

15. **Sometimes, he tells short stories.**

CD-104309 • © Carson-Dellosa   61

Name _____   **Sentences**

Sentences

A **sentence** is a group of words that tells a complete idea.
  Example: Sentence   We traveled around the United States.
            Not a sentence   Around the United States.

**Write *S* if the words below make a sentence. Write *NS* if they do not make
a sentence.**

__S__   I. We went to Texas.

__NS__ 2. Saw the Alamo in San Antonio.

__S__   3. Colorado is a beautiful state.

__NS__ 4. Tall mountains and cool air.

__S__   5. I would like to live there.

__S__   6. We also saw California.

__NS__ 7. The beautiful ocean.

Write words of your own to complete each sentence. Answers will vary.

8. This summer, _____

9. Our dog Bingo _____

10. One day, _____

62   CD-104309 • © Carson-Dellosa

Name _____   **Sentences**

Sentences

A **sentence** is a group of words that tells a complete idea.
  Example: Sentence   Our tennis team won the match.
            Not a sentence   Our tennis team.

**Draw a line to match the beginning of each sentence on the left with the
correct end of each sentence on the right.**

I. Basketball   make a basket.

2. Two teams   the most points wins.

3. Each team   is fun.

4. You try to   play each other.

5. The team with   has five players.

Write words of your own to complete each sentence. Answers will vary.

6. The sport _____

7. My team _____

8. During one game, _____

9. After the game, _____

CD-104309 • © Carson-Dellosa   63

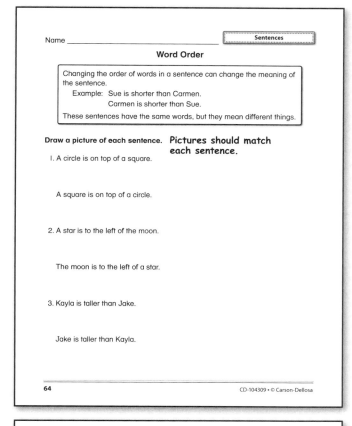

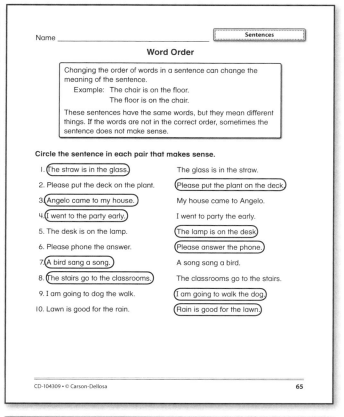

Name _____

Declarative Sentences

A **declarative sentence** makes a statement. Declarative sentences begin with a capital letter and end with a period (.).
Examples: Statements   Mario likes to ride in airplanes.
                                Tim likes to ride in the car.
                Not Statements   What do you like to ride in?
                                Where do you like to go?

Write S for each sentence that makes a statement. Write NS for each sentence that does not make a statement.

__S__ 1. Earth has seven big areas of land.

__S__ 2. The largest continent is called Asia.

__NS__ 3. Which is the smallest?

__S__ 4. One continent is too cold for people to live.

__NS__ 5. How cold is it?

__S__ 6. Many people live in Asia.

__NS__ 7. Where do you live?

__S__ 8. The United States is part of North America.

Write each declarative sentence with a capital letter and a period.

9. i enjoy going to new places __I enjoy going to new places.__

10. i always bring my camera __I always bring my camera.__

Write your own statement with a capital letter and a period.

11. __Answers will vary.__

Name _____

Interrogative Sentences

An **interrogative sentence** asks a question. An interrogative sentence begins with a capital letter and ends with a question mark (?).
Examples: What did you have for lunch?
                Did you have a sandwich?

Write Q for each sentence that asks a question. Write NQ for each sentence that does not ask a question.

__Q__ 1. What time do you eat lunch?

__NQ__ 2. Jerry ate a pickle.

__Q__ 3. Who ate an orange?

__NQ__ 4. Lunch is my favorite meal.

__Q__ 5. Where is the lunchroom?

__Q__ 6. Do you smell the pie?

__Q__ 7. What kind of vegetable is this?

__NQ__ 8. Please set the table.

Write each interrogative sentence with a capital letter and a question mark.

9. do we eat lunch at noon
__Do we eat lunch at noon?__

10. should i bring my lunch
__Should I bring my lunch?__

11. can Jephta buy her lunch
__Can Jephta buy her lunch?__

12. will we sit at the same table
__Will we sit at the same table?__

Name _____

Interrogative Sentences

An **interrogative sentence** asks a question. An interrogative sentence begins with a capital letter and ends with a question mark (?).
Examples: Who is playing the piano?
                Is Tim singing?

Write Q for each sentence that asks a question. Write NQ for each sentence that does not ask a question.

__Q__ 1. Are you in the band?

__NQ__ 2. Collin plays the flute.

__Q__ 3. Who plays the drums?

__Q__ 4. Have you heard of Buddy Holly?

__Q__ 5. Do you like music?

__NQ__ 6. A piano has 88 keys.

__Q__ 7. Does a violin have four strings?

__NQ__ 8. Lisa plays electric guitar.

Write each interrogative sentence with a capital letter and a question mark.

9. what kind of music do you like
__What kind of music do you like?__

10. do you sing
__Do you sing?__

11. can you make music with a spoon
__Can you make music with a spoon?__

12. is Katie in a band
__Is Katie in a band?__

Name _____

Interrogative Sentences

An **interrogative sentence** asks a question. An interrogative sentence begins with a capital letter and ends with a question mark (?).
Examples: Which color do you like best?
                Who is painting?

Write Q for each sentence that asks a question. Write NQ for each sentence that does not ask a question.

__Q__ 1. Do you like to draw?

__Q__ 2. What do you draw?

__NQ__ 3. I like to use a pencil.

__Q__ 4. Do you have colored pencils?

__Q__ 5. Will you show me how to draw?

__NQ__ 6. I want to draw a horse.

__Q__ 7. Is drawing easy for you?

__Q__ 8. Which pencil is yours?

Write each interrogative sentence with a capital letter and a question mark.

9. does John like to paint
__Does John like to paint?__

10. which color is his favorite
__Which color is his favorite?__

Write your own interrogative sentence with a capital letter and a question mark.

11. __Answers will vary.__

Name _____

Exclamatory Sentences

An **exclamatory sentence** shows strong feeling. It starts with a capital letter and ends with an exclamation mark (!). Some exclamatory sentences are only one or two words long.
Examples: Wow!
What a great movie!

Write E for each sentence that shows strong feeling. Write NE for each sentence that does not show strong feeling.

__E__ 1. You are doing a great job!

__NE__ 2. That is a nice shirt.

__E__ 3. There is a mouse!

__NE__ 4. Is the wind blowing?

__E__ 5. Boo!

Write each exclamatory sentence with a capital letter and an exclamation mark.

6. ouch
Ouch!

7. what an amazing sunset
What an amazing sunset!

8. this is the best soup ever
This is the best soup ever!

72 — CD-104309 • © Carson-Dellosa

Name _____

Exclamatory Sentences

An **exclamatory sentence** shows strong feeling. It starts with a capital letter and ends with an exclamation mark (!). Some exclamatory sentences are only one or two words long.
Examples: Hooray!
You did a great job!

Write E for each sentence that shows strong feeling. Write NE for each sentence that does not show strong feeling.

__NE__ 1. What did they say?

__E__ 2. It is a boy!

__NE__ 3. Thank you for the card.

__E__ 4. I am so happy for you!

__E__ 5. That is wonderful news!

Write each exclamatory sentence with a capital letter and an exclamation mark.

6. watch out
Watch out!

7. i had a great day
I had a great day!

Write your own exclamatory sentence with a capital letter and an exclamation mark.

8. **Answers will vary.**

CD-104309 • © Carson-Dellosa — 73

Name _____

Imperative Sentences

An **imperative sentence** gives a command. An imperative sentence can end in an exclamation mark (!) or a period (.).
Examples: Clean your room!
Be good.

Write I for each sentence that gives a command. Write NI for each sentence that does not give a command.

__NI__ 1. It is time to wake up.

__I__ 2. Put on your clothes.

__NI__ 3. Breakfast is ready.

__NI__ 4. Can you be ready in five minutes?

__I__ 5. Remember your homework!

__NI__ 6. The bus leaves soon.

__I__ 7. Have a good day!

__NI__ 8. When will you be home?

Draw a line to match the words on the left with the words on the right to make imperative sentences.

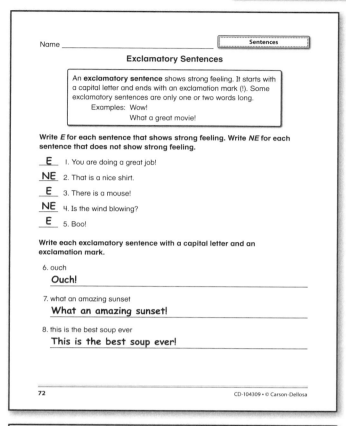

9. Remember — a good job!
10. Be — your umbrella.
11. Find — nice!
12. Do — your seat, please.

74 — CD-104309 • © Carson-Dellosa

Name _____

Imperative Sentences

An **imperative sentence** gives a command. An imperative sentence can end in an exclamation mark (!) or a period (.).
Examples: Pick up your toys.
Look out!

Write I for each sentence that gives a command. Write NI for each sentence that does not give a command.

__I__ 1. Show your mom your painting.

__NI__ 2. She will love it!

__I__ 3. Tell her how you made it.

__NI__ 4. Has your dad seen it?

__I__ 5. Make him a painting.

__NI__ 6. You could make a card.

__NI__ 7. Cards are great gifts.

__I__ 8. Get started!

Draw a line to match the words on the left with the words on the right to make imperative sentences.

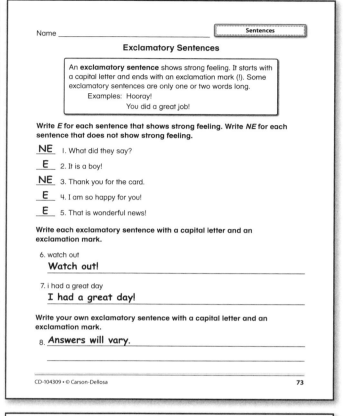

9. Start — out the trash.
10. Take — your best.
11. Do — moving!
12. Sit, — Bingo!

CD-104309 • © Carson-Dellosa — 75

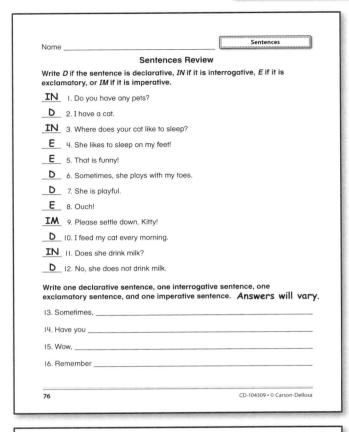

Name _____   Sentences

Sentences Review

Write *D* if the sentence is declarative, *IN* if it is interrogative, *E* if it is exclamatory, or *IM* if it is imperative.

IN 1. Do you have any pets?

D 2. I have a cat.

IN 3. Where does your cat like to sleep?

E 4. She likes to sleep on my feet!

E 5. That is funny!

D 6. Sometimes, she plays with my toes.

D 7. She is playful.

E 8. Ouch!

IM 9. Please settle down, Kitty!

D 10. I feed my cat every morning.

IN 11. Does she drink milk?

D 12. No, she does not drink milk.

Write one declarative sentence, one interrogative sentence, one exclamatory sentence, and one imperative sentence. **Answers will vary.**

13. Sometimes, _____

14. Have you _____

15. Wow, _____

16. Remember _____

76   CD-104309 • © Carson-Dellosa

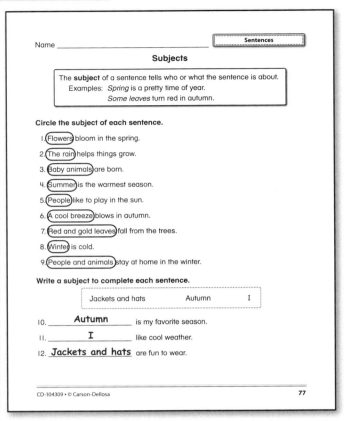

Name _____   Sentences

Subjects

> The **subject** of a sentence tells who or what the sentence is about.
> Examples: *Spring* is a pretty time of year.
> *Some leaves* turn red in autumn.

Circle the subject of each sentence.

1. (Flowers) bloom in the spring.

2. (The rain) helps things grow.

3. (Baby animals) are born.

4. (Summer) is the warmest season.

5. (People) like to play in the sun.

6. (A cool breeze) blows in autumn.

7. (Red and gold leaves) fall from the trees.

8. (Winter) is cold.

9. (People and animals) stay at home in the winter.

Write a subject to complete each sentence.

| Jackets and hats | Autumn | I |

10. ____**Autumn**____ is my favorite season.

11. _____**I**_____ like cool weather.

12. __**Jackets and hats**__ are fun to wear.

CD-104309 • © Carson-Dellosa   77

Name _____   Sentences

Subjects

> The **subject** of a sentence tells who or what the sentence is about.
> Examples: *Birds* are flying in the sky.
> *The cat* is sleeping.

Circle the subject of each sentence.

1. (Katie) saw a book on a chair.

2. (She) took the book to her teacher.

3. (Her teacher) asked the class about the book.

4. (Nobody) was missing the book.

5. (Rick and Tina) walked with Katie to the office.

6. (The lost-and-found box) was in the office.

7. (They) gave the book to an office helper.

8. (The office helper) was happy.

9. (The book) was his!

Write a subject to complete each sentence.

| Mr. Thomas | Mystery stories | He |

10. __**Mr. Thomas**__ is the office helper.

11. _____**He**_____ likes to read at lunch.

12. __**Mystery stories**__ are his favorite books.

78   CD-104309 • © Carson-Dellosa

Name _____   Sentences

Subjects

> The **subject** of a sentence tells who or what the sentence is about.
> Examples: *Bo and Mary* walked to the park.
> *A dog* ran by them.

Draw a picture of the subject of each sentence. **Pictures should match each sentence.**

1. The telephone rang twice before Ann answered.

2. The sun is bigger than the moon.

3. Rita and Javier are in the band at Jefferson School.

4. Bananas taste better than apples.

5. Five pennies equal a nickel.

CD-104309 • © Carson-Dellosa   79

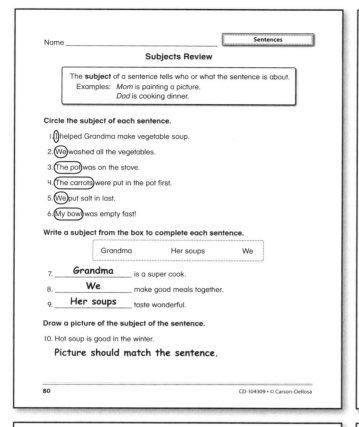

Name _____

| Sentences |

Subjects Review

The **subject** of a sentence tells who or what the sentence is about.
Examples: *Mom* is painting a picture.
Dad is cooking dinner.

Circle the subject of each sentence.

1. (I) helped Grandma make vegetable soup.
2. (We) washed all the vegetables.
3. (The pot) was on the stove.
4. (The carrots) were put in the pot first.
5. (We) put salt in last.
6. (My bowl) was empty fast!

Write a subject from the box to complete each sentence.

| Grandma | Her soups | We |

7. **Grandma** is a super cook.
8. **We** make good meals together.
9. **Her soups** taste wonderful.

Draw a picture of the subject of the sentence.

10. Hot soup is good in the winter.

Picture should match the sentence.

80   CD-104309 • © Carson-Dellosa

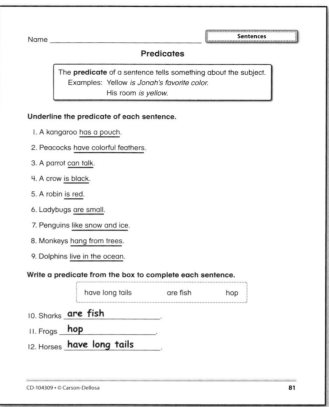

Name _____

| Sentences |

Predicates

The **predicate** of a sentence tells something about the subject.
Examples: Yellow *is Jonah's favorite color.*
His room *is yellow.*

Underline the predicate of each sentence.

1. A kangaroo has a pouch.
2. Peacocks have colorful feathers.
3. A parrot can talk.
4. A crow is black.
5. A robin is red.
6. Ladybugs are small.
7. Penguins like snow and ice.
8. Monkeys hang from trees.
9. Dolphins live in the ocean.

Write a predicate from the box to complete each sentence.

| have long tails | are fish | hop |

10. Sharks **are fish** .
11. Frogs **hop** .
12. Horses **have long tails** .

CD-104309 • © Carson-Dellosa   81

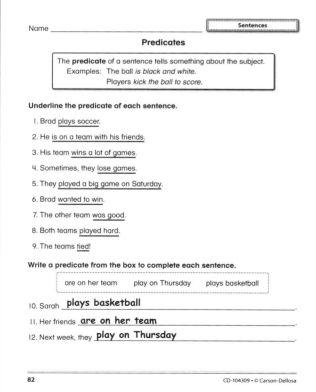

Name _____

| Sentences |

Predicates

The **predicate** of a sentence tells something about the subject.
Examples: The ball *is black and white.*
Players *kick the ball to score.*

Underline the predicate of each sentence.

1. Brad plays soccer.
2. He is on a team with his friends.
3. His team wins a lot of games.
4. Sometimes, they lose games.
5. They played a big game on Saturday.
6. Brad wanted to win.
7. The other team was good.
8. Both teams played hard.
9. The teams tied!

Write a predicate from the box to complete each sentence.

| are on her team | play on Thursday | plays basketball |

10. Sarah **plays basketball** .
11. Her friends **are on her team** .
12. Next week, they **play on Thursday** .

82   CD-104309 • © Carson-Dellosa

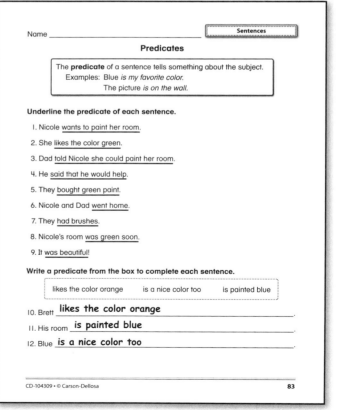

Name _____

| Sentences |

Predicates

The **predicate** of a sentence tells something about the subject.
Examples: Blue *is my favorite color.*
The picture *is on the wall.*

Underline the predicate of each sentence.

1. Nicole wants to paint her room.
2. She likes the color green.
3. Dad told Nicole she could paint her room.
4. He said that he would help.
5. They bought green paint.
6. Nicole and Dad went home.
7. They had brushes.
8. Nicole's room was green soon.
9. It was beautiful!

Write a predicate from the box to complete each sentence.

| likes the color orange | is a nice color too | is painted blue |

10. Brett **likes the color orange** .
11. His room **is painted blue** .
12. Blue **is a nice color too** .

CD-104309 • © Carson-Dellosa   83

Name _____

Predicates Review

Underline the predicate of each sentence. Write it on the line.

1. My family <u>went on a trip</u>.
   went on a trip

2. We <u>packed the car</u>.
   packed the car

3. My mom and dad <u>drove</u>.
   drove

4. My brother and I <u>sang songs in the backseat</u>.
   sang songs in the backseat

5. We all <u>had fun</u>.
   had fun

Write your own predicate to finish each sentence. Answers will vary.

6. The huge elephant _____.

7. A rose _____.

8. My shoes _____.

9. Butterflies _____.

10. In the summer, I _____.

84   CD-104309 • © Carson-Dellosa

Name _____

Capitalization

> The first word in a sentence begins with a **capital letter**.
> Examples: The cat is orange and white.
>   An apple is round.
> A person's title and his or her first and last name should begin with a **capital letter**.
> Examples: Chris Parker
>   Ms. Lewis

Circle each letter that needs to be capitalized.

1. My friends (J)ane (S)mith and (C)ody (N)orton are in my class.
2. (O)ur teacher is (M)r. (C)ole.
3. Today, I went to see (D)r. (C)ollier.
4. (T)his jacket belongs to (M)ary (D)gosdin.
5. (H)as anyone seen (J)ack (U)., today?
6. My mom called (A)unt (S)usan yesterday.

Answer each question with a person's name. Answers will vary.

7. Who is your teacher? _____

8. Who is one of your friends? _____

9. Who is your neighbor? _____

10. Who do you know owns a dog? _____

CD-104309 • © Carson-Dellosa   85

Name _____

Capitalization

> Days, months, and names of cities, states, and provinces should begin with a **capital letter**.
> Examples: Friday, October 12
>   Portland, Oregon

Circle each letter that needs to be capitalized.

1. School starts on (S)eptember 2 this year.
2. My favorite day is (T)uesday.
3. We visited (A)ustin, (T)exas, in (M)ay.
4. Brian lives in (N)ew (Y)ork (C)ity, (N)ew (Y)ork.
5. On (W)ednesday, (D)ecember 9, we will see a play.
6. Next (M)onday is my birthday.

Answer each question with a day, month, or name of a city or state.

7. When is your birthday? _____ **Answers will vary.**

8. What town or city do you live in? _____

9. What is today? _____

10. Where would you like to visit? _____

86   CD-104309 • © Carson-Dellosa

Name _____

Capitalization

> The first word and all important words in book and movie titles should begin with a **capital letter**.
> Examples: *The Magic School Bus*
>   *Dictionary of Animals*

Circle each letter that needs to be capitalized.

1. (T)he (L)ittle (R)ed (E)ngine
2. (L)ily goes to (R)ome
3. (P)laying the (G)uitar
4. (G)uide to (D)inosaurs
5. (L)earn to (M)ake a (K)ite
6. (B)ingo (C)hases (S)ticks

Answer each question with a book or movie title. Answers will vary.

7. What is your favorite book? _____

8. What is your favorite movie? _____

9. What book are you reading now? _____

10. What was the last movie you saw? _____

CD-104309 • © Carson-Dellosa   87

Name _____

Capitalization Review

Circle each letter that needs to be capitalized.

1. Our school has (f)riday off.

2. (i) am reading a book called (s)aving the (o)cean.

3. I would like to visit (b)oulder, (c)olorado.

4. (w)ill (m)r. (n)elson be there?

5. (t)he talent show is on (j)uly 22.

6. I am glad that (j)ason (f)loyd and (a)shley (h)arris will be there.

7. This letter will go to (s)pring, (a)rizona.

8. (m)y sister's birthday is (j)anuary 23.

Answer each question. **Answers will vary.**

9. What country do you live in? _____

10. Who is sitting next to you? _____

11. When is your teacher's birthday? _____

12. What is a book about an animal? _____

Name _____

Ending Punctuation

Every sentence ends with a **punctuation mark**.

A declarative sentence ends with a **period**.
   Example: My name is Sherry.

An interrogative sentence ends with a **question mark**.
   Example: What is your name?

An exclamatory sentence ends with an **exclamation mark**.
   Example: Here I am!

An imperative sentence ends with either a period or an exclamation mark.
   Examples: Please close the window.
                    Wow!

Write the correct ending punctuation mark for each sentence.

1. The sky is getting dark **.**

2. Can I watch your game **?**

3. I cannot believe it **!**

4. You found me **!**

5. Will you be at the party **?**

6. Tina is taking a dance class **.**

7. Laura is my older sister **.**

8. The clock has stopped **.**

9. What do you want for dinner **?**

10. Not again **!**

11. This is easy **!**

12. The lettuce is fresh **.**

13. Do you want to play a game **?**

14. What a beautiful song **!**

Name _____

Ending Punctuation

A declarative sentence ends with a **period**.
An interrogative sentence ends with a **question mark**.
An exclamatory sentence ends with an **exclamation mark**.
An imperative sentence ends with either a **period** or an **exclamation mark**.

Write the correct ending punctuation mark for each sentence.

1. What size shoe do you wear **?**

2. The kitchen is painted yellow **.**

3. When will you be home **?**

4. I cannot carry this box much longer **!**

5. Do you have a pencil **?**

6. The parrot repeated what Lucy said **.**

7. We need an umbrella right now **!**

8. Ida likes to sleep with the fan on **.**

9. Did you find this shell at the beach **?**

10. What fun **!**

11. What did you think of the movie **?**

12. I would like some water **.**

13. Artie went for a walk **.**

14. I counted over 100 bees **!**

Name _____

Contractions

A **contraction** is made when two words are put together. Letters are taken out and an apostrophe is put in their place.
   Examples: does + not = *doesn't*
                    would + not = *wouldn't*
Some contractions do not follow this rule.
   Example: will + not = *won't*

Match each word with its contraction.

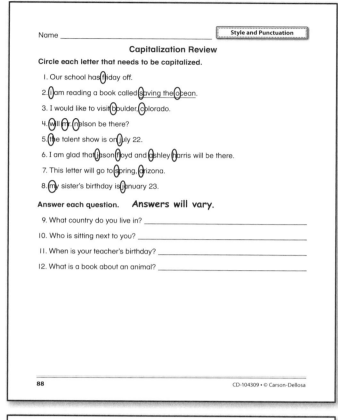

1. is not
2. had not
3. does not
4. cannot
5. has not
6. do not
7. could not
8. will not
9. are not
10. would not
11. did not
12. was not
13. have not
14. were not

aren't
hasn't
don't
won't
can't
wouldn't
wasn't
haven't
didn't
hadn't
weren't
couldn't
isn't
doesn't

Name _____

Contractions

A **contraction** is made when two words are put together.
Letters are taken out and an apostrophe is put in their place.
Some contractions are made with a pronoun + a verb.
Examples: she + will = *she'll*   I + am = *I'm*
he + is = *he's*   we + are = *we're*

Match each word with its contraction.

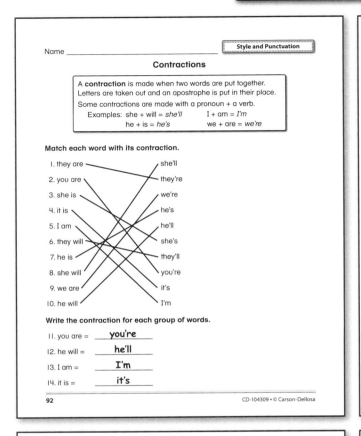

1. they are   she'll
2. you are   they're
3. she is   we're
4. it is   he's
5. I am   he'll
6. they will   she's
7. he is   they'll
8. she will   you're
9. we are   it's
10. he will   I'm

Write the contraction for each group of words.

11. you are = **you're**
12. he will = **he'll**
13. I am = **I'm**
14. it is = **it's**

CD-104309 • © Carson-Dellosa

Name _____

Contractions

A **contraction** is made when two words are put together.
Letters are taken out and an apostrophe is put in their place.

Write the contraction for each word or group of words.

1. cannot = **can't**
2. they are = **they're**
3. do not = **don't**
4. will not = **won't**
5. she is = **she's**

Write a contraction to finish each sentence.

6. She **didn't** know what time it was.
   (did not)
7. Tom **can't** go to the game.
   (cannot)
8. I think **I'm** going to need a coat today.
   (I am)
9. You **won't** believe it!
   (will not)
10. It sounds like **you're** not feeling well.
    (you are)
11. Please **don't** slip on the ice!
    (do not)
12. Vonda says **it's** time to go home.
    (it is)

CD-104309 • © Carson-Dellosa

Name _____

Contractions

A **contraction** is made when two words are put together.
Letters are taken out and an apostrophe is put in their place.

Write the contraction for each group of words.

1. is not = **isn't**
2. does not = **doesn't**
3. would not = **wouldn't**
4. he is = **he's**
5. she will = **she'll**

Write a contraction to complete each sentence.

6. We **haven't** seen the movie.
   (have not)
7. Ryan **wasn't** able to visit Aunt Anne.
   (was not)
8. He said **he'll** be there at 2:00 p.m.
   (he will)

Write your own sentence with the contraction for each word or group of words. Answers will vary.

9. cannot: _____

_____

10. will not: _____

_____

CD-104309 • © Carson-Dellosa

Name _____

Possessives

A **possessive** word tells who or what owns something. To make a word possessive, you add an apostrophe and the letter *s*.
Examples: The book's cover is pink. → the cover belongs to the book
Mary's shoe has a bow. → the shoe belongs to Mary

Write the possessive form of each word.

1. Mark   **Mark's**
2. uncle   **uncle's**
3. grandmother   **grandmother's**
4. city   **city's**
5. boat   **boat's**
6. Kate   **Kate's**
7. child   **child's**
8. flower   **flower's**

Write the possessive form of the word to complete each sentence.

9. The **candle's** flame was orange.
   (candle)
10. I read **Andy's** story.
    (Andy)
11. The **fruit's** peel was tough.
    (fruit)
12. Sasha likes the **character's** laugh.
    (character)

CD-104309 • © Carson-Dellosa

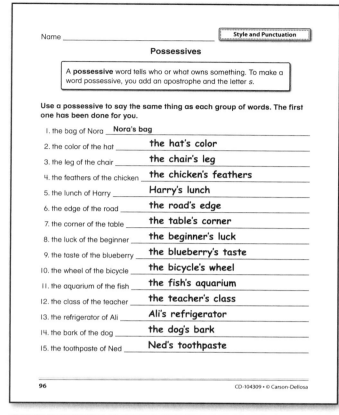

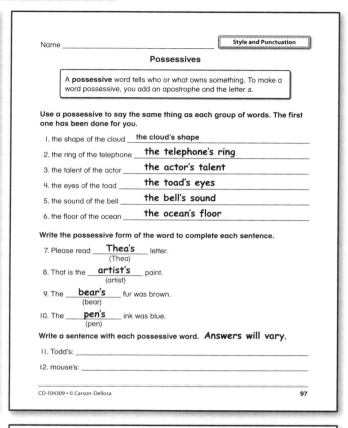

Page 96 — Possessives

Name _____ Style and Punctuation

Possessives

A **possessive** word tells who or what owns something. To make a word possessive, you add an apostrophe and the letter *s*.

Use a possessive to say the same thing as each group of words. The first one has been done for you.

1. the bag of Nora — Nora's bag
2. the color of the hat — the hat's color
3. the leg of the chair — the chair's leg
4. the feathers of the chicken — the chicken's feathers
5. the lunch of Harry — Harry's lunch
6. the edge of the road — the road's edge
7. the corner of the table — the table's corner
8. the luck of the beginner — the beginner's luck
9. the taste of the blueberry — the blueberry's taste
10. the wheel of the bicycle — the bicycle's wheel
11. the aquarium of the fish — the fish's aquarium
12. the class of the teacher — the teacher's class
13. the refrigerator of Ali — Ali's refrigerator
14. the bark of the dog — the dog's bark
15. the toothpaste of Ned — Ned's toothpaste

96   CD-104309 • © Carson-Dellosa

Page 97 — Possessives

Name _____ Style and Punctuation

Possessives

A **possessive** word tells who or what owns something. To make a word possessive, you add an apostrophe and the letter *s*.

Use a possessive to say the same thing as each group of words. The first one has been done for you.

1. the shape of the cloud — the cloud's shape
2. the ring of the telephone — the telephone's ring
3. the talent of the actor — the actor's talent
4. the eyes of the toad — the toad's eyes
5. the sound of the bell — the bell's sound
6. the floor of the ocean — the ocean's floor

Write the possessive form of the word to complete each sentence.

7. Please read ____Thea's____ letter. (Thea)
8. That is the ____artist's____ paint. (artist)
9. The ____bear's____ fur was brown. (bear)
10. The ____pen's____ ink was blue. (pen)

Write a sentence with each possessive word. **Answers will vary.**

11. Todd's: _____
12. mouse's: _____

CD-104309 • © Carson-Dellosa   97

Page 98 — Proofreading

Name _____ Editing

Proofreading

Reading your sentences to check for mistakes is called **proofreading**. Check for mistakes in spelling, capital letters, and punctuation marks.

Example: Before proofreading   Vanessa and bill are swingin (3 mistakes)
          Corrected   Vanessa and Bill are swinging.

Each sentence has an incorrect or missing capital letter. Draw a circle around the letter that needs to change.

1. (m)y family climbed aboard the boat.
2. We sailed into the (S)unset.
3. My sister, (s)imone, sat with the captain.
4. His name was (m)r. Chang.
5. We (A)ll had fun.

Each sentence has an incorrect or missing punctuation mark. Circle the mistake and write the correct punctuation mark.

6. What time did the boat leave( ) **?**
7. We will be back when it is dark( ) **.**
8. Mom and I sat up front( ) **?**
9. It was outstanding( ) **!**
10. Can we go again( ) **?**

Each sentence has one misspelled word. Circle the misspelled word. Then, spell it correctly.

11. The wind pushed the (bot) through the water. **boat**
12. We ate dinner on (tha) boat. **the**

98   CD-104309 • © Carson-Dellosa

Page 99 — Proofreading

Name _____ Editing

Proofreading

Reading your sentences to check for mistakes is called **proofreading**. Check for mistakes in spelling, capital letters, and punctuation marks.

Proofread each sentence. Look for mistakes with capital letters and punctuation marks. Circle each mistake.

1. I'm glad for our (F)riendship.
2. My grandfather worked on the railroad(?)
3. Is (b)ob going to pick strawberries( )
4. (p)lease put a stamp on the letter( )
5. (i) live on (h)udson (s)treet.
6. Our (N)eighborhood is quiet.

Each sentence has one misspelled word. Circle the misspelled word. Then, spell it correctly.

7. I will (slep) well tonight. **sleep**
8. The apple tasted (gud). **good**

Write each sentence correctly.

9. what time is it
   What time is it?
10. sue lives in orlando, florida
   Sue lives in Orlando, Florida.

CD-104309 • © Carson-Dellosa   99

Answer Key

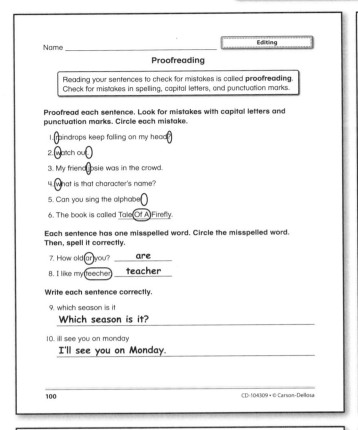

Name _____   Editing

Proofreading

Reading your sentences to check for mistakes is called **proofreading**.
Check for mistakes in spelling, capital letters, and punctuation marks.

Proofread each sentence. Look for mistakes with capital letters and punctuation marks. Circle each mistake.

1. (R)aindrops keep falling on my head(.)

2. (W)atch ou(t)

3. My friend (J)osie was in the crowd.

4. (W)hat is that character's name?

5. Can you sing the alphabe(t)

6. The book is called Tale (Of A) Firefly.

Each sentence has one misspelled word. Circle the misspelled word. Then, spell it correctly.

7. How old (ar) you? _____ **are**

8. I like my (teecher) _____ **teacher**

Write each sentence correctly.

9. which season is it
   Which season is it?

10. ill see you on monday
    I'll see you on Monday.

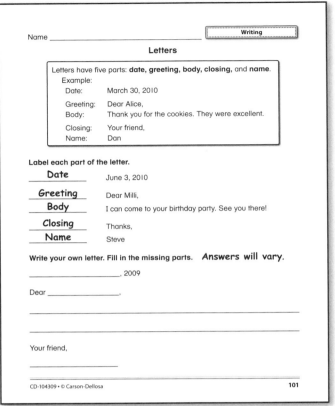

Name _____   Writing

Letters

Letters have five parts: **date, greeting, body, closing,** and **name**.
Example:
Date: March 30, 2010
Greeting: Dear Alice,
Body: Thank you for the cookies. They were excellent.
Closing: Your friend,
Name: Dan

Label each part of the letter.

Date _____ June 3, 2010

Greeting _____ Dear Milli,

Body _____ I can come to your birthday party. See you there!

Closing _____ Thanks,

Name _____ Steve

Write your own letter. Fill in the missing parts.   **Answers will vary.**

_____, 2009

Dear _____,

_____

_____

Your friend,

_____

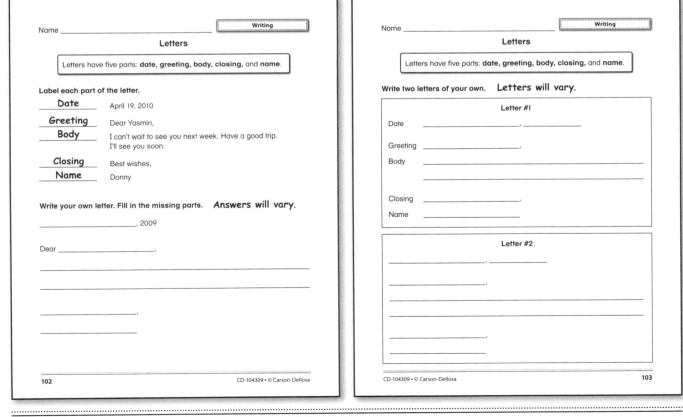

Name _____   Writing

Letters

Letters have five parts: **date, greeting, body, closing,** and **name**.

Label each part of the letter.

Date _____ April 19, 2010

Greeting _____ Dear Yasmin,

Body _____ I can't wait to see you next week. Have a good trip. I'll see you soon.

Closing _____ Best wishes,

Name _____ Donny

Write your own letter. Fill in the missing parts.   **Answers will vary.**

_____, 2009

Dear _____,

_____

_____

_____,

_____

Name _____   Writing

Letters

Letters have five parts: **date, greeting, body, closing,** and **name**.

Write two letters of your own.   **Letters will vary.**

Letter #1
Date _____, _____
Greeting _____,
Body _____
_____
Closing _____,
Name _____

Letter #2
_____, _____
_____,
_____
_____
_____,
_____

Congratulations!

receives this award for

Signed

Date

's

article

state-of-being verb

exclamatory sentence

© CD

!

adjective

plural noun

interrogative sentence

© CD

?

verb

proper noun

declarative sentence

© CD

.

noun

pronoun

past tense verb

© CD

imperative sentence	subject	predicate	contraction
palace	friends	hamsters	computer
farm	dentist	Ms. Jones	Mr. Allen
The Corner Store	Three Circle Ranch	Monday	Father's Day

cook	smiled	held	was
build	walked	made	are
finish	played	sang	am
December	sleep	gave	is

funny

tiny

wonderful

longest

© CD

© CD

© CD

© CD

have

sour

beautiful

younger

© CD

© CD

© CD

© CD

has

hungry

sweet

coolest

© CD

© CD

© CD

© CD

were

green

tall

warmer

© CD

© CD

© CD

© CD

carlos

october 14, 2009

will not

I'm

a

alice baker

won't

do not

an

the little red engine

cannot

she will

the

mr. chang

can't

it's

the bark of
the dog

closing

Put on
your
clothes.

here I am

Andy's

body

Wow!

my birthday
is in
november

the socks
of Ned

greeting

The ball is
black and
white.

swimming
is fun

Thea's

date

name

Can I
come?